BUDDHIST MONASTIC LIFE

BUDDHIST MONASTIC LIFE

according to the texts of
the Theravāda tradition

MOHAN WIJAYARATNA

Translated by Claude Grangier
and Steven Collins

with an Introduction by
Steven Collins

The right of the University of Cambridge to print and sell all manner of books was granted by Henry VIII in 1534. The University has printed and published continuously since 1584.

CAMBRIDGE UNIVERSITY PRESS

Cambridge
New York Port Chester Melbourne Sydney

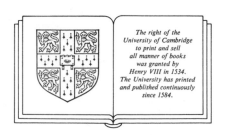

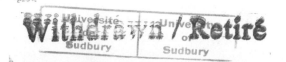

Published by the Press Syndicate of the University of Cambridge
The Pitt Building, Trumpington Street, Cambridge CB2 1RP
40 West 20th Street, New York, NY 10011, USA
10 Stamford Road, Oakleigh, Melbourne 3166, Australia

First published 1990

Printed in the United States of America

Library of Congress Cataloging-in-Publication Data

Wijayaratna, Môhan.
[Moine bouddhiste. English]
Buddhist monastic life : according to the texts of the Theravāda tradition / by Mohan Wijayaratna : translated by Claude Grangier and Steven Collins : with an introduction by Steven Collins.
p. cm.
Translation of: Le moine bouddhiste.
Includes bibliographical references.
ISBN 0-521-36428-0. – ISBN 0-521-36708-5 (pbk.)
1. Monasticism and religious orders, Buddhist. 2. Theravāda Buddhism. I. Title.
BQ6084.W5513 1990
294.3'657–dc20 90-33129
CIP

British Library Cataloguing in Publication Data

Wijayaratna, Mohan
Buddhist monastic life.
1. Buddhist monasteries. Theravāda Buddhist life
I. Title II. Le Moine bouddhiste selon les textes du Theravāda. *English*
294.3444

ISBN 0-521-36428-0 hardback
ISBN 0-521-36708-5 paperback

Contents

Acknowledgments

This book was originally published in French under the title *Le Moine bouddhiste selon les textes du Theravāda* (Editions du Cerf, Paris 1983). I am grateful to my friends Miss Marie-Thérèse Drouillon and Miss Brigitte Carrier who helped me to write it and Messrs. Bernard Lauret and Nicolas Zed who helped me to publish it. I am also grateful to the staff of the library of the Collège de France for their helpful and courteous service.

In regard to this English edition, I wish to add a word of sincerest thanks to both translators who have done their work with utmost care, and to the Cambridge University Press for publishing it. Very specially I am thankful to Professor Steven Collins for his Introduction, Glossary and Index.

I must take this opportunity of recording my deep sense of gratitude to Professor Richard Gombrich for the encouragement and inspiration he gave me from the beginning of the realisation of this English edition.

Let us hope that this small book will be useful to the reader in Buddhist studies.

Paris
25 August 1989

Mohan Wijayaratna

Acknowledgments

[illegible]

[illegible]

[illegible]

Introduction

Buddhist Monasticism

The monastic tradition of Buddhism is probably the oldest in the world, and has certainly been the most widespread, both geographically and culturally. The traditional dates for the Buddha given in Western scholarship are c.566–486 B.C.[1]: the order he founded has existed for two and a half thousand years. Although by the medieval period the Buddhist monastic order had all but disappeared from India, by that time it had been established in almost every other part of Asia. During the centuries following the Buddha's death various different "schools" of Buddhism arose; this book describes the ideal monastic life envisaged by one of them, the Theravāda or "Way of the Elders."[2] These ideals are preserved in the Pali canonical texts and commentaries and have been followed in India from the ancient to early medieval periods (a small modern presence remains in Bengal, and, by recent reintroduction, in Nepal); in Sri Lanka (formerly Ceylon) from the third century B.C.; and in mainland Southeast Asia (what are now Burma, Thailand, Laos and Cambodia) from medieval times until the present day. Alas, the twentieth century has not been kind to Buddhism: modern governments in mainland China, Tibet, Vietnam, North Korea, Laos and Cambodia have attempted either to destroy the religion altogether or at least put very severe restrictions on the institutional possibilities for practicing it.

As Dr. Wijayaratna explains in Chapter 1, the Buddha and

his disciples are said to have been one of a number of groups of religious mendicants in ancient India; Buddhist texts call such a group a *gaṇa*, and each had its *gaṇācariya*, "group teacher" or "leader." It might have been the Buddha's slightly older contemporary Mahāvīra, the founder of Jainism, who was the first to convert such a group into a monastic Community (*saṅgha*) by means of a codified Monastic Rule; but Jain tradition holds that its earliest texts have been lost, and we cannot recover the precise chronology and nature of the earliest Jain monasticism. Buddhist texts say that the Buddha first established the Community of monks; later, apparently with reluctance and after the intercession of his faithful companion Ānanda, he granted the wish of his aunt and foster-mother Mahāpajāpatī and established the Community of nuns. We know from inscriptions and texts that the order of nuns existed in India and elsewhere in South Asia until the medieval period, but it seems to have died out then.[3] In Buddhist monastic law, the ordination of any new nuns requires the presence of a number of other properly ordained monks and nuns. In different Theravāda countries at different times, the order of monks has sometimes declined so much that there have not been enough properly ordained monks to continue ordaining new members; but the ordination lineage has been reestablished with the help of monks from other countries. This did not happen with the order of nuns. Although subsequently there have been women following what Dr. Wijayaratna calls "the path of inner progress," their status in both monastic and civil law has been that of laypersons who practice an extended version of lay Buddhist ethics by following eight or ten Precepts rather than the usual five.[4] Thus while the Monastic Rule for nuns is extant in the texts, as are many stories about individual nuns, unless and until some way is found to reestablish the nun's Community in Theravāda countries, these texts are of historical interest only, and do not provide an actual code of behavior for women Buddhists today. For this reason, although in this book Dr. Wijayaratna often writes about the nuns and their rules, this aspect of the subject is not so thoroughly explored as are the ideals for monks.[5]

THERAVĀDA BUDDHIST LITERATURE[6]

The texts used by Dr. Wijayaratna are all in Pali, and fall into two groups, the Canon and the commentaries. The Canon is divided into three "baskets" (*piṭaka*): that of the Monastic Rule or Disciplinary Code (*Vinaya-piṭaka*), the Discourses or Sermons of the Buddha (*Sutta-piṭaka*), and the systematic psychological and philosophical texts of "Further Doctrine" (*Abhidhamma-piṭaka*). These texts were at first preserved orally; all Buddhist schools speak of a number of Councils or "Communal Recitations" (*saṅgīti*) said to have taken place in the first few centuries of Buddhist history; unfortunately, these accounts are for the most part mutually incompatible. The Theravāda version holds that the first two "baskets" were recited at the first council, held immediately after the Buddha's death, while the third was finally closed at a third council held under Emperor Aśoka in the third century B.C. It is also held that the tradition of commentarial works was begun at an early period (indeed the Canon itself contains material of the commentarial genre); the mission sent out by Aśoka to introduce Buddhism to Ceylon is said to have brought with it both Canon and commentaries. Both kinds of "text" were still preserved orally, until they were written down for the first time in the latter part of the first century B.C.; at some point, presumably before this, the commentaries were translated into the contemporary language of Ceylon (Sinhala). The commentarial works extant, however, date from a later period; those used in this book are attributed to two great Indian scholar-monks, Buddhaghosa and Dhammapāla, in the fifth and sixth centuries A.D. Both of these authors state, however, that they were basing their Pali commentaries very closely on earlier texts preserved by the monastic lineage in Ceylon named after its main monastery in Anurādhapura, the Mahāvihāra.

Dr. Wijayaratna draws most of his data from the *Vinaya-* and *Sutta-piṭakas*, with occasional use of the commentaries on them. The *Vinaya* has two main sections, called *Sutta-Vibhaṅga* and *Khandhaka*, along with a third and probably later appendix called *Parivāra*. The *Sutta-Vibhaṅga* contains the *Pā-*

timokkha, which is the basic list of rules for monks (227) and nuns (311), embedded in a text made up of stories — particularly of the circumstances that led to the Buddha's promulgation of each rule — and an old word-by-word commentary on each rule. The organisation of the rules is explained and discussed in Chapter 8; the *Pātimokkha* itself is recited in an important monastic ceremony which takes place on the days of the full and new moon, called *Uposatha* (see Chapter 7, pp. 123–24). The *Khandhaka* has two parts, the *Mahāvagga* and *Cullavagga*, which contain a variety of materials arranged thematically, including parts of the Buddha's biography, various rules and observances (such as "On Robe Material" and "On Medicines"), stories of monks in different areas, and accounts of the founding of the nuns' Order and of the first two Councils. The *Sutta-piṭaka* contains five collections of texts, each known as a *Nikāya*. The first four (*Dīgha, Majjhima, Saṃyutta,* and *Aṅguttara*) contain discourses arranged in accordance with their length and/or subject matter, most of which are attributed to the Buddha. The fifth (*Khuddaka*) is a miscellaneous collection of texts, some clearly early, others clearly late; of particular importance to Dr. Wijayaratna's account, especially in Chapter 1 on the members of the earliest Community, are the poems attributed to monks and nuns, the *Theragāthā* and *Therīgāthā*, and the stories collected in Dhammapāla's commentary on them.

How Reliable are the Texts?

It seems to me useful to divide Theravāda Buddhist history into three periods; these chronological layers are not, obviously, to be taken as separate realities in actual history, but simply reflect the different kinds of evidence which are available to us.[7] The first or "early" period lasts from the time of the Buddha (whenever that was) to that of Aśoka. Some of Aśoka's inscriptions mention Greek kings, whom we can date with confidence, and so his reign, c.268–239 B.C., provides the first really secure historical data we have for Buddhism, and indeed for any ancient Indian history. We have no evidence of any kind which can be dated before Aśoka; we must make inferences from his inscriptions, from the texts (whose extant form is due to the later period), and perhaps also from the material remains of later times. From the time of Aśoka onwards, in the second or "middle" period, in addition to an increasingly large amount of textual materials, we have inscriptions, paintings, sculptures and other material remains to supplement and on occasion correct what the texts tell us. Neither material remains nor texts – which include sources in indigenous languages other than Pali – are as extensive as those to which historiographers of the classical or medieval West apply their skills, but they still provide the basis for writing history in a straightforward sense (not that this is ever easy, of course). The third of "modern" period refers to those recent centuries in which we have first-hand reports from western travelers, officials of imperial governments, anthropologists and others, as well as the modern records kept by indigenous rulers and bureaucracies. The first work of this period is the still useful account by the English sailor Robert Knox of his enforced sojourn in Ceylon from 1659–79 (reprinted in Knox 1956–7). In very recent times the study of Theravāda Buddhism has been particularly rich in ethnographies and modern histories written by both western and indigenous observers.

How far is it possible to use the extant texts as evidence for the early period? Obviously, we cannot conclude that because something is *not* described in the texts, it could not have happened; but this kind of argument will never establish anything positively. The question is: what use can we make of what the texts do tell us? Let me start by quoting two leading contemporary scholars of Theravāda. Richard Gombrich, in a review of the French version of this book, wrote:

> It is a modest, straightforward account of what the Pali Canon tells us of how Buddhist monks and nuns were supposed to live. Oddly enough, no such account has been published before. Most authors who have written on the Sangha

> have concerned themselves largely with the Buddha's doctrine and monastic spirituality, giving pride of place to the inner life. Sukumar Dutt's admirable pioneering work was an attempt to write an early *history* of the Sangha, relating it to its antecedents and speculating on its development; scholars have tended to accept most of his conclusions without going back to the evidence . . . Dr. Wijayaratna is content to give us a synchronic picture . . . [He] refuses to discuss chronology or stratification, but takes the canonical account at face value (without, however, saying that he believes it). I find his approach fruitful. What he has shown is that the sources are predominantly consistent. Whether they go back to the Buddha is of course another matter; but when one has read this book it is no longer possible to maintain that the Pali *Vinaya* and *Sutta Piṭakas* are a hotchpotch of material drawn from several centuries.[8]

Heinz Bechert, in the bibliography to a brief overview article on the Buddhist monastic Community, writes: "unfortunately, the existing monographs on the early *Saṃgha* are of limited use only, because their authors, who have not understood the rules of Vinaya as a legal system, concentrate on historical aspects and often propose problematic theories." He also mentions Sukumar Dutt's work as an example of this.[9]

Neither of these two writers, nor I, wish to belittle Dutt's contribution to the subject: on the contrary, his books remain important and helpful, and deal with many more topics than can be discussed here. But it is useful to take his work as an example of a general principle: if scholarship is to advance, it is impossible to rely on such secondary sources as if they have established once and for all the truth about their subject. We must always go back to the primary sources. To exemplify the point, let me take one aspect of Dutt's most important and influential speculation, concerning the nature and evolution of the earliest Saṅgha. Dutt first proposed his account specifically as "a theory," indeed a "very bold" one, but over the years it has assumed the role of a received wisdom.[10] Although he acknowledges (1962, p. 57) that "in the *Vinaya-*

piṭaka the Bhikkhu-saṅgha appears not as a body of wanderers but as a settled cenobitical society," he argues that this was a development from an original stage where "settled life in a monastery is not contemplated at all, and the ideal life for a Bhikkhu is set out to be a free, unsocial, eremitical one" (1960, p. 112). In support of this he cites the well-known phrase used by the Buddha when sending out the first sixty monks to preach, "let not two of you go the same way" (Vin I 21). For Dutt, "the eremitical ideal indicated here . . . [is] a life of solitude and hardship" (1960, p. 112). It was, in his view, the Rainy Season Retreat, when monks stayed together in one place for the three or four months' duration of the monsoon season, which was the turning point "from wandering to settled life." But as Dr. Wijayaratna explains in Chapter 2, what the texts actually contain is more complex: while they do say that moving from place to place was an important part of the early Community's lifestyle, they also say that the Buddha accepted a park donated as a residence by King Bimbisāra of Magadha very soon after his Enlightenment and founding of the Order. This park was on the outskirts of the town of Rājagaha, and was specifically chosen as somewhere neither too far from nor too close to lay society. When members of the Community traveled, they usually went from one such park or monastery to another. Similarly, in the story of the first institution of the Rainy Season Retreat (see pp. 19ff. below), the text does not tell us that *all* monks and nuns were always traveling, continuing throughout the monsoon, but only that some monks in one place (Rājagaha) did so on one occasion, and were criticised for it. The injunction to travel alone forms part of an injunction to travel and spread the Teaching "for the good of the many. . . . out of compassion for the world" (cited on p. 19 and elsewhere in this book); in the context it obviously means that the original small band of monks, on their first journey, should split up to cover as much ground as possible, without wasting manpower. It says nothing about a general mode of life prescribed for all monks all of the time.[11] Thus Dr. Wijayaratna's conclusion seems to me impeccable, and describes what the texts actually contain rather than the "history" which Dutt (and others) have presumed to read from them: although "some scholars think that the institution of the Rainy Season Retreat served as a bridge between two periods in the history of the Buddhist monkhood: wandering and sedentary life . . . we are not dealing here with a transformation, nor with two different stages; the institution of the Retreat served rather to connect two different styles of life" (p. 21 below).

Both before and after the adoption of the Rains Retreat by Buddhism (which was already the practice of other ascetic groups), members of the *saṅgha* lived both itinerant and sedentary lives. In the earliest "missionary" days, most monks are said to have traveled constantly to spread the Buddha's message; but they are also said to have stayed in one place for periods of time. Apart from those who were ill or old (see p. 30), the practical details of monastic organization required some members of the Order to remain in monasteries and other residences of the Community (see, for example, Chapters 2, 3 and 4 on the appointment of monks to oversee the assigning of lodgings, robes and food). In fact, to accept the myth of a transition "from eremitical to cenobitical life" is, as the Christian terminology shows, to impose on Buddhist monastic history categories derived from the received wisdom about the Christian tradition – which is itself equally legendary and unhistorical.[12] The word "eremitical," like "hermit," derives from a Greek term used to refer to the fact of living in places away from normal human habitation, notably the deserts and mountains of Egypt and other areas in what is now called the Middle East; "cenobitical" means having a "shared" or "common life," and is used to describe those who lived together under a Monastic Rule. Since some (but by no means all) of the Christian "dwellers in the wilderness" lived alone for some or all of the time, the eremitical life came to be contrasted in that tradition with the cenobitical. (The question of solitude in Buddhist monasticism is discussed in Chapter 7.) But this opposition is not that between traveling and remaining in one place; in fact most of the "Desert Fathers" in early Christian history, whether they lived alone or with others, did not travel, apart from pilgrimages and going to visit others. When the earliest Buddhist monks are described as traveling to preach, apart from the first group of sixty they are frequently pictured as doing so in groups. So Dutt's "theory" coalesces three quite separate issues, about which the texts have many different things to say: living alone or living with others, traveling or staying in one place, and living far from or close to other human habitations.

What Dr. Wijayaratna does here, then, is to let the texts speak plainly and clearly for themselves. His judicious selection and presentation of the evidence shows that the ideal system of monasticism they present is, in general, a single and coherent one; we are not presented with a series of historical layers and an evolution from one thing to another. The question still remains, of course, whether the picture of the early Saṅgha presented in the texts is historically accurate; this raises much bigger and more difficult problems, which apply to the study of any religious tradition: that of the overall chronology and provenance of the canonical texts, and of the relationship between textual ideals and actual practice. These are subjects on which, naturally and rightly, opinions differ. In Buddhism, as elsewhere, it is possible to use archaeological and epigraphical data to balance the textual accounts,[13] and also to compare Buddhist textual sources with those of other traditions, notably Jainism.[4] In the case of what I called the "early," pre-Aśokan period, however, apart from what very little we can infer about Buddhist monastic life from Aśoka's inscriptions, the texts are all we have. For this period, therefore, I agree with what Richard Gombrich has said elsewhere, again referring to the French version of this book: "the *Vinaya* as it stands is of a piece, and if we refuse to believe its own account of the Sangha's development – as of course we can – we are left with no certain knowledge of the subject" (1988, p. 93). One might say, with perhaps some exaggeration, that if any parts of the *Vinaya-piṭaka* are accepted to be early, then, in the absence of external evidence, it might all be; and equally, if any parts are adjudged to be late, then it might all be late. In this case as with almost all of the Pali Canon, I believe, attempts to demonstrate historical layers based solely on internal evidence produce not historical scholarship, but merely a certain kind of inept and *a priori* literary criticism.

In the Introduction to the French version of this book, Dr. Wijayaratna made clear his own attitude to the evidence provided by the textual tradition, and it is in this spirit that the book should be read:

> This work will not attempt a critical analysis of the opinions found in the *Sutta-piṭaka,* nor to discover the date at which one or another *Nikāya* was collected. With regard to the *Vinaya-piṭaka,* it is probable that even in the area of monastic discipline some rules were drawn up and arranged later, after the Buddha's death; nevertheless the Buddha is regarded as having established the rules of the Community. It is likely, in fact, that the principles and precepts of the Community were subject to elaboration during the first few centuries of its existence. We will take the following view; whenever we find that the origin of a particular rule is attributed to the Buddha, we may conclude *either* that at the time when the definitive version of the code of discipline was drawn up, this rule was thought to be a precept established by the Buddha himself, *or* that at that time the disciples felt the need to present or regard such a rule as coming from him. Whether or not one or another precept was in fact established by the Buddha, what is important from our point of view is the sense and interpretation it is given by Theravāda monasticism.
>
> In the following pages, the intention is simply to give an account of the discourses and rules which the Theravādins regard as the Doctrine (*Dhamma*) and the Discipline (*Vinaya*) of their tradition . . . On occasion we will make use of the Pali commentaries in order to come to a better understanding of some canonical passages. It is true that quite a stretch of time separates the Pali Canon from the commentaries on it: the canonical texts come from the third century B.C., whereas the Pali commentaries as we now have them belong to the fifth century A.D. Nonetheless, the Pali commentaries are valuable, for two reasons. The first is historical: the Pali com-

mentaries did not appear suddenly in the fifth century. They were based on the Old Commentaries and on the interpretations given by the Theravādin Elders and teachers, which had been handed down from generation to generation. The second is an issue of interpretation: Theravāda monastic tradition must be seen, in my opinion, not from the point of view of the Mahāyāna, of the Vajrayāna, or of Hinduism, but from that of the Theravāda itself. For that reason it is necessary to take into account both the opinions and attitudes specific to the Theravāda, and its tradition of interpretation.

Suggestions for Further Reading

THE VINAYA-PIṬAKA

References to the Pali text of the *Vinaya-piṭaka* in this work, as in that of almost all other scholars of Buddhism, are to the roman script version edited by H. Oldenberg, and published by the Pali Text Society, London (last reprinted 1964–82). Parts of it were translated by Oldenberg and T.W. Rhys Davids, in *Vinaya Texts*, Sacred Books of the East vols. 13, 17 and 20 (last reprinted by Motilal Banarsidass 1982–4). Miss I.B. Horner translated the whole text as *Book of the Discipline* Parts 1–6, Sacred Books of the Buddhists vols. X, XI, XII, XIV, XX, XXV (last reprinted by the Pali Text Society 1966–83). References are to the volume and page number of the Pali text: unfortunately, the text and translations of the *Vinaya* are not easy to collate, since Oldenberg edited the text in an order different from the traditional canonical one, whereas the translations follow the canonical order. The canonical divisions and order were described earlier; the following table is intended to help readers, particularly those without knowledge of Pali, to check references and study particular parts of the text further:

(O = Oldenberg's text; IBH = Horner's translation; O/RhD = Oldenberg and Rhys Davids' translation.)
The *Sutta-vibhaṅga* (i) Rules for monks (*bhikkhu-vibhaṅga*) = O

vols. III and IV pp. 1–207; IBH Parts 1, 2 and 3 pp. 1–155; O/RhD (the *Pātimokkha* rules only) Part 1 pp. 1–69.
The *Sutta-vibhaṅga* (ii) Rules for nuns (*bhikkhunī-vibhaṅga*) = O vol. IV pp. 211–351; IBH Part 3 pp. 156–426; not translated by O/RhD.
The *Mahāvagga* = O vol. I; IBH Part 4; O/RhD Parts 1 pp. 73–355, and 2 pp. 1–325.
The *Cullavagga* = O vol. II; IBH Part 5; O/RhD Part 2 pp. 329–439, and Part 3.
The *Parivāra* = O vol. V; IBH Part 6; not translated by O/RhD.

All of these works contain valuable introductions, notes and appendices.

HISTORICAL AND INTRODUCTORY WORKS (IN ENGLISH).

E.W. Adikaram (1953) *Early History of Buddhism in Ceylon,* (M.D. Gunasena, Colombo)
S. Bandaranayake (1974) *Sinhalese Monastic Architecture* (E.J. Brill, Leiden)
H. Bechert (1979) *Buddhism and Society* (Wheel no. 265, Buddhist Publication Society, Kandy)
______ (1987) "*Saṃgha*: an overview," in Eliade (1987)
H. Bechert and R.F. Gombrich (eds.) (1984) *The World of Buddhism* (Thames and Hudson, London)
S. Collins (1988) "Monasticism, Utopias and Comparative Social Theory" *Religion* vol. 18, pp. 101–135
J. Dhirasekara (1981) *Buddhist Monastic Discipline* (M.D. Gunasena, Colombo)
S. Dutt (1924, 1960) *Early Buddhist Monachism* (1st. ed. Routledge and Kegan Paul, London; 2nd. ed. Asia Publishing House, London)
______ (1962) *Buddhist Monks and Monasteries of India* (Allen and Unwin, London)
M. Eliade (ed.) (1987) *Encyclopedia of Religion* (Macmillan, New York)
N. Falk (1980) "The Case of the Vanishing Nuns: the Fruits of Ambivalence in Ancient Indian Buddhism," in N. Falk and R. Gross (eds.) *Unspoken Worlds: Women's Religious Experiences in Non-Western Cultures* (Harper and Row, New York)
E. Frauwallner (1956) *The Earliest Vinaya and the Beginnings of Buddhist Literature* (ISMEO, Rome)
W. Geiger (1960) *Culture of Ceylon in Mediaeval Times* (Harrassowitz, Wiesbaden)
R.F. Gombrich (1986) review of M. Wijayaratna, *Le Moine Bouddhiste*, in *Religion*, vol. 16 pp. 387–88

——— (1988) *Theravāda Buddhism a Social History from Ancient Benares to Modern Colombo* (Routledge and Kegan Paul, London)
R.A.L.H. Gunawardana (1979) *Robe and Plough: Monasticism and Economic Interest in Early Medieval Sri Lanka* (University of Arizona Press)
J. Holt (1981) *Discipline: the Canonical Buddhism of the Vinayapiṭaka* (Motilal Banarsidass, Delhi)
J. Knox (1956–7) *An Historical Relation of Ceylon* (Ceylon Historical Journal VI, 1–4)
E. Lamotte (1988) *History of Indian Buddhism* (English translation, Peeters Press, Université Catholique de Louvain)
B.C. Law (1939–40) "Bhikshunis in Indian Inscriptions," in *Epigraphia Indica*, vol. 25, pp. 31–34
G.P. Misra (1972) *The Age of Vinaya* (Munshiram Manoharlal, Delhi)
K.R. Norman (1983a) *Pali Literature* (Harrassowitz, Wiesbaden)
——— (1983b) "The *Pratyeka-buddha* in Buddhism and Jainism," in P. Denwood and A. Piatigorsky (eds.) *Buddhist Studies Ancient and Modern* (Curzon Press, London)
P. Olivelle (1974) *The Origin and Early Development of Buddhist Monachism* (M.D. Gunasena, Colombo)
C. Prebish (1975) *Buddhist Monastic Discipline: the Sanskrit Prātimokṣa Sūtras of the Mahāsaṃghikas and Mūlasarvastivādins* (The Pennsylvania State University Press, University Park and London)
W. Rāhula (1974) *The Heritage of the Bhikkhu* (Grove Press, New York)
N. Ratnapāla (1974) *The Katikāvatas: Laws of the Buddhist Order of Ceylon from the Twelfth Century to the Eighteenth Century* (Kitzinger, Munich)
F.E. Reynolds and C.S. Hallisey (1987) "Buddhism: an overview," in Eliade (1987)
G. Schopen (1984) "Filial Piety and the Monk in the Practice of Indian Buddhism," in *T'oung Pao* vol. LXX, pp. 110–126
——— (1985) "Two Problems in the History of Indian Buddhism," in *Studien zur Indologie und Iranistik*, Heft 10, pp. 9–47
——— (1989) "The Stūpa Cult and the extant Pali Vinaya," in *Journal of the Pali Text Society*, vol. XIII, pp. 83–100
H.L. Seneviratne (1987) "Saṃgha and Society," in Eliade (ed.) (1987)
I. Strenski (1984) "On Generalized Exchange and the Domestication of the *Sangha*," in *Man* n.s. 18, pp. 463–77

RECENT ETHNOGRAPHIC WORKS

L. Bloss (1987) "The Female Renunciants of Sri Lanka: the *Dasasilmattawa*," in *Journal of the International Association of Buddhist Studies*, vol. 10, 1, pp. 7–31
J. Bunnag (1973) *Buddhist Monk, Buddhist Layman* (Cambridge University Press, Cambridge)
M.B. Carrithers (1983) *The Forest Monks of Sri Lanka* (Oxford University Press, Delhi)

H-D Evers (1972) *Monks, Priests and Peasants* (E.J. Brill, Leiden)
R.F. Gombrich (1971) *Precept and Practice* (Oxford University Press, London)
R.F. Gombrich and G. Obeyesekere (1988) *Buddhism Transformed* (Princeton University Press, Princeton)
R. Gothóni (1982) *Modes of Life of Theravāda Monks* (Studia Orientalnia 52, Helsinki)
I. Jordt, (1989) "Bhikkhuni, Thilashin, Mae-chii," in *Crossroads* (Centre for Southeast Asian Studies, Northern Illinois University, Dekalb), vol. 4, no. 1, pp. 31–39
K. Malalgoda (1976) *Buddhism in Sinhalese Society, 1750–1900* (University of California Press)
E.M. Mendelson (1975) *Sangha and State in Burma* (ed. J. Ferguson, Cornell University Press, Ithaca)
E. Nissan (1984) "Recovering Practice: Buddhist Nuns in Sri Lanka," in *South Asia Research*, vol. 4, 1, pp. 32–49
M.E. Spiro (1970) *Buddhism and Society* (Allen and Unwin, London)
D. Swearer (1976) *Wat Haripuñjaya* (Scholars Press, Montana)
S.J. Tambiah (1970) *Buddhism and the Spirit Cults of Northeast Thailand* (Cambridge University Press, Cambridge)
——— (1976) *World Conqueror and World Renouncer* (Cambridge University Press, Cambridge)
——— (1984) *The Buddhist Saints of the Forest and the Cult of Amulets* (Cambridge University Press, Cambridge)
B.J. Terwiel (1975) *Monks and Magic* (Scandanavian Institute of Asian Studies, Lund)

Notes to the Translation

In this translation we have tried to render in English as clearly as we could the content and style of *Le Moine Bouddhiste*. In consultation with Dr. Wijayaratna, we have changed the wording and order of some passages, incorporated most footnotes into the text, omitted some repetitions and most references to French secondary sources, provided references to English works instead of French where possible, corrected some typographical errors and references to Pali texts, and added the brief Appendix 3 on the Precepts; Dr. Wijayaratna has provided some new references and the new Appendix 1, with a fuller account of the Order of Nuns. Endnotes in square brackets are translation notes. Abbreviations used follow the scheme of the *Critical Pali Dictionary* (published by the Royal Danish Academy of Sciences and Letters: see the Epilegomena to Vol. 1); texts referred to are the editions of the Pali Text Society, London. The word *pāli/pāḷi* is printed in Anglicized form, without diacritical marks.

I should like to thank Patrick Olivelle and Gregory Schopen for helpful comments on an earlier draft of this Introduction.

Steven Collins
Montréal, September 1989

Endnotes

1. There is another reckoning which would move these dates forward to 448–368 B.C.
2. For a discussion of these early schools see Lamotte (1988); and for a succinct explanation and definition of the Theravāda tradition as a monastic entity see Gombrich (1988) pp. 110–2.
3. See Falk (1980), Gunawardana (1979) pp. 37–39 and Law (1939–40).
4. These precepts are given in Appendix 3, and cf. Appendix 2, pp. 166–67, 170–71.
5. The bibliography given here includes some ethnographic materials on women's "monastic" practice in modern Buddhism.
6. See K.R. Norman (1983a) for a fuller account.
7. The first two of these are similar to those identified by Heinz Bechert (e.g. 1979) as "early" and "traditional"; but his criterion for division and designation is the relation of the monastic community to society, and my third, "modern" period does not correspond exactly to his third, "modernist" one. My choice of terms is not intended, as are Bechert's and also those used by Reynolds and Hallisey (87), to suggest anything about the character of Buddhism in different periods, but merely to delineate three historical layers in terms of the evidence we have for them.
8. Gombrich (1986) pp. 387–88, italics in original.
9. Bechert (1987) p. 40. The two authors I have cited here have

collaborated to produce an excellent reference work on the Buddhist monastic order in all traditions, which is also beautifully illustrated: Bechert and Gombrich (1984). The sections in this book called 'Buddhism in Ancient India' and 'Theravāda Buddhism' provide the best available introduction to the history of the Saṅgha in South and Southeast Asia.

10. See the Preface to Dutt (1924) p. x, where the work is also said to have been written as a thesis in 1916, a time obviously when serious Buddhist studies had only recently begun. In the revised edition of this work, (1960) p. ix, the wording was changed to 'somewhat bold' and the date of writing omitted; and in Dutt (1962), the hypothetical nature of the suggestion is forgotten, the account being presented with little hesitation as historical fact. Other scholars have usually used the 1960 and 1962 versions of Dutt's work.
11. For a brief but trenchant critique of Dutt along these lines, see Dhirasekara (1981) pp. 6ff., who cites some appropriate remarks of I.B. Horner.
12. This is particularly clear in Dutt (1924 and 1960) Chapter 5, which takes the four-fold classification of monks from the Rule of St. Benedict as its model. For references to scholarship showing the legendary nature of this version of Christian monastic history, see Collins (1988) pp. 106–108 and notes 22–27.
13. This has been done recently with great creativity by Gregory Schopen: see, for example 1984, 1985 and 1989.
14. See, for example, K.R. Norman's (1983b) discussion of the word and concept *pacceka-buddha* (Sanskrit *pratyeka-buddha*).

Chapter 1

The origin of the Community

> *As a lotus is attached neither to water nor to mud, so the sage is attached neither to sensual pleasures nor to the world . . .*
>
> (Sn 625).

Buddhism first arose as a movement of "renouncers." In common with a number of other such movements at the time, it was opposed to Brahmanism, which placed highest value on lay life and its rituals; and so the core of this new movement consisted of monks and nuns. But it was not long before lay people, both men and women, gathered around them as their supporters and followers. One can therefore distinguish two kinds of disciples of the Buddha: monks and nuns (*les religieux*[1]), and lay people.

The word *saṅgha,* which literally means a crowd or gathering, came to refer specifically to the Community of monks and nuns in the terminology of Theravāda monasticism. In Pali texts the term *saṅgha* does not include lay-followers; these are included in the expression *cattāro parisā,* "the fourfold assembly": *bhikkhu* (monks), *bhikkhunī* (nuns), *upāsaka* and *upāsikā* (male and female layfollowers). The monastic Community is made up of two groups: *bhikkhu-saṅgha* (the order of monks) and *bhikkhunī-saṅgha* (the order of nuns); together they are called *ubhatosaṅgha,* "the twofold community" (M III 255). To refer to the entire Community, in any and every place, another term is used: *cātudissa bhikkhusaṅgha,* "the Community of the four quarters." This phrase is found in the *Vinaya* texts and in ancient inscriptions, to symbolize the Community's common spirit and common ownership of property.

According to the Pali Canon, the monastic Community was first established in Benares, in the Deer Park, after the first discourse of the Buddha to the five ascetics, Kondañña, Vappa, Bhaddiya, Mahānāma and Assaji (Vin I 12). A few days later, a wealthy young man named Yasa and some of his friends joined the new religious movement; they were soon followed by another group of young men, equally eager to become disciples of the Buddha (Vin I 19). Thus by the end of the first year the Community numbered several hundred members. Many of them, like the five ascetics, had previously been members of another religious group, but left it in order to become disciples of the Buddha. Great ascetic leaders such as Uruvela-Kassapa, Gāya-Kassapa, and Nadī-Kassapa, along with their disciples, abandoned their practice of fire-sacrifice to join the young movement (Vin I 31–34). Before becoming the Buddha's disciples, Pippali-Mānava, a young and wealthy brahmin (later to become the Arahant Mahā-Kassapa Thera), and his wife Bhaddā-Kapilānī (who later became a famous nun, the Arahant Bhaddā-Kapilānī) had been members of another religious sect (S II 215). Sivaka (Th 183–184), a brahmin from Rājagaha, had already renounced lay life and joined a group of *paribbājakā* (wandering religious mendicants); Vijaya (Th 92), a brahmin from Sāvatthi, had lived as a lone ascetic in the forest. Bhaddā-Kuṇḍalakesā, the young daughter of a very wealthy family, joined the Nigaṇṭha (Jain) community after a very unhappy marriage, and became a Jain orator of great reknown. She later told the story of the useless austerities which she had practiced as a Jain nun (Thī 107–111, Thī-a 99ff., A I 25, Mp 200). It was on being defeated by the Arahant Sāriputta Thera in a public debate that she became a member of the Buddha's Community. (Such public debates were not unusual among wandering mendicants in ancient North India.) Nanduttarā, a brahmin woman, was also a disciple of Jainism and given to the practice of austerities, but was persuaded to join the Community when she heard the Arahant Moggallāna Thera preach (Thī 87–91).

Vacchagotta, whom we meet in several discourses in the *Nikāya* texts (A I 160, 180; M I 481, 483; S III 257, IV 401), had been a famous wandering mendicant, like Sāriputta and Moggallāna, who were known as Upatissa and Kolita; later they became the two greatest disciples of the Buddha (Vin I 38).

All these people were renouncers, members of one or another sect or religious group; so they had already renounced lay life before becoming disciples of the Buddha. This means that Buddhism had no influence on their original renunciation. The majority of the Buddha's disciples in these early days, however, abandoned lay life in order to enter the Community. Of the sixty disciples gathered around the Buddha in the first six months, fifty-five were young laymen who moved directly to religious life in the Community. The Buddha's teaching had therefore directly motivated their renunciation.

At first, many of those who renounced lay life to join the Community were young. Indeed Buddhist monasticism encouraged people to renounce family life as early as possible. A young monk called Soṇa Kuṭikanna (cf. Vin I 194; Ud. 57), a pupil of Mahā-Kaccāna Thera, came from Avanti to Sāvatthi to see the Buddha. The Buddha had a long talk with him, noted with satisfaction that the young monk had a good knowledge of the Teaching, and asked him how long he had been in the Community. "A year, Blessed One," answered Soṇa. The Buddha then asked him, "Why did you wait so long before joining the Community?" The young monk answered, "Blessed One, I had been aware for a long time of the suffering and vanity of worldly life, but family problems prevented me from leaving it."

In this new "religion," the first stage of the monastic life was regarded as a period of training. This is why young people were always more welcome than older ones: when someone was old and feeble, he or she did not have the same strength to devote to renunciation and to the practice of the virtues. A passage from the Canon comments, "It is difficult to find these five important qualities in people who have renounced lay life in old age: they are not good at speaking, learning, understanding, preaching, and remembering" (A III 77). At that time the prevalent opinion was, on the contrary, that the religious life was best suited to older people who had put family life behind them. When a person grew older he or she was "doomed" to the religious life. For example, one day some young Buddhist nuns were bathing in the river Aciravatī (nowadays the Rāpti). Some courtesans mocked them: "What are you doing, venerable ladies, leading a life of purity (*brahmacariya*) while you are young? Is it not better to enjoy yourselves? Wait until you are old to embrace the religious life: that way you will know both kinds of life, one now and the other later" (Vin I 293, IV 278).

Nonetheless, despite this general opinion, many of the Buddha's disciples were young people. To join him, most of them had abandoned wealth, a life of luxury, and even a young wife. Young men needed their parents' permission to renounce lay life, even if they were married; but parents were not always happy to let them go. When Raṭṭhapāla asked his parents for permission to join the Community, they refused, saying "Why do you want to become a monk? Your hair is still black and you are still young." Raṭṭhapāla went without food and drink until he obtained permission. Once it was given, he renounced his home and received from the Community both the minor (*pabbajjā*) and the major (*upasampadā*) Ordinations. One day his father saw him walking in the street and said sadly to his wife, "Look, our only son, our beloved son! He has given up everything and taken on the practice of these shaven-headed priestlings" (M II 54–62). Such words reflect the sadness and disapproval of parents who had lost their son or daughter to the new religion. The Commentary to the *Dhammapada* (IV 164ff.) tells us that a rich Brahman woman called Rūpasāri (the mother of Sariputta Thera) complained that the Buddhist monkhood had taken all her children from her, one after another.

Among the Buddha's disciples there were many who had renounced lay life because they were attracted to his doctrine. After they heard him preach, they wanted to lead the religious life that the Master had showed them, and so renounced family life. The *Mahāvagga* (Vin I 23) tells the story of some rich young men used to "the good life" (*bhaddavagiya*). One day these young men, about thirty in all, had gone for a picnic in the forest with their wives. One of them, who had no wife, had brought along a courtesan. When everyone was merry, she took some valuables, jewels and other things, and stole away. The young men went to look for her and chanced upon the Buddha sitting at the foot of a tree, He said, "Tell me, young men, what is better for you, to look for this woman or to look for yourselves?" The result of this brief discussion was that the young men were persuaded to renounce lay life and enter the Community.

Two wealthy young men, Raṭṭhapāla (M II 61) and Sudinna Kalandakaputta (Vin II 11ff.), also renounced wealth and lay life simply on hearing the Buddha's words. A young merchant by the name of Puṇṇa (or Puṇṇika) came to the town of Sāvatthi on business and had occasion to hear the Buddha's doctrine; he then renounced lay life (Th 70, Th-a I 156). Young Migajāla, one of Visākhā's sons, who used to go to the monastery of Jetavana every day with his mother, left home after he heard the Doctrine preached (Th 417–422, Th-a I 452), as also did Rājadatta, one of the chief merchants in the town of Rājagaha, on the very day when he want to talk with the Buddha at Veḷuvana monastery (Th 315–319,1 Th-a I 402). In the same way, Kappa (Th 567–576, Th-a I 521), regional governor of the Magadha country, Kuṇḍadhāna (Th 62, Th-a I 146), a learned brahmin from Sāvatthi, Dhammavaniya (Th 67, Th-a I 151), a son of good family, Kāsi-Bhāradvāja (Sn p. 12, Pj II 131), a rich brahmin from Dakkhiṇagiri, all renounced lay life to become monks simply on hearing the Buddha speak. Similarly, Sīhā, the niece of general Sīha from Vesāli, decided to renounce lay life on hearing a discussion between the Buddha and the venerable Sāriputta Thera (Thī 77–81). Vimalā, daughter of a courtesan from Vesāli, saw the venerable Moggallāna Thera, fell in love with him and decided to follow him. When she heard him preach she renounced lay life (Thī 72–76). Khemā, wife of King Bimbisāra, took the same decision on hearing the Buddha's words (Thī 139–144). Ambapāli, a famous courtesan from Vesāli, decided to renounce lay life when she heard a sermon preached by her son, the venerable Vimala-Koṇḍañña Thera (Thī 252–270). Puṇṇā, a young woman of twenty, who lived in Rājagaha, was persuaded by a sermon given by the nun Mahā-Pajāpatī Gotamī Therī (Thī 3, Thī–a 9f.).

All these people had had a life of comfort and luxury. They renounced the world to become monks and nuns under the influence of the Buddha's doctrine. If someone who is used to luxury chooses to renounce everything in order to live according to a philosophy or doctrine, he or she probably feels an intellectual need to do so. There is no doubt that the people mentioned above wanted to find a way to lead a more satisfying life. Their outlook was transformed when they heard the Master's doctrine; his words provoked in them a mental evolution or revolution which led them to change their way of life completely. No abnormal or miraculous phenomenon was involved. These people were persuaded that the Buddha's doctrine was the only path to deliverance or salvation, and simply reoriented their lives accordingly and renounced everything else.

The canonical texts tell us that many people renounced lay life because of the Buddha's personality. We might describe this as a form of "hero-worship"; that is, admiration for an inspiring character. In all religions and in all societies there are people who follow the example of an influential leader. According to the canonical texts, the Buddha had a very powerful personality. He was graceful, gentle, always in good spirits, full of energy and ever smiling. He was "the Blessed One, he who brings and spreads joy, whose senses are tranquil and whose mind is at peace, the supreme self-conqueror, he who lives in peace, the hero who has tamed himself, who keeps watch over himself and keeps a tight rein on his senses" (D I 88; II 16; M II 133–136). The disciples of Uruvela-Kassapa said, "Truly he is handsome, this Great Ascetic" (Vin I 25), an opinion shared by the people of Rājagaha (Vin II 195). Some brahmins were particularly struck by the Buddha's physical appearance (M II 135; Sn 837). An old brahmin called Māgandiya thought the Buddha so handsome that he wanted him to marry his daughter, who was a great beauty herself. The Buddha rejected the offer (Sn 835, Pj II 542–4, Dhp-a III 193–7), and soon afterwards the brahmin renounced lay life to become his disciple. This refusal created a lifelong enemy of Miss Māgandiyā, who later married a crown prince and tried for revenge (Dhp-a I 202, 210ff.). Vakkali, another learned brahmin, was so moved by the Buddha's charm that he followed him in the street for a long time, and finally renounced lay life to become a disciple of this "attractive man." Even after he had become a monk, he could not stop looking at the Buddha, who advised him on the contrary to concentrate on his Doctrine rather than on his body (Th 350–354, Th-a I 420).

It is perhaps for this very reason that some non-Buddhist ascetics did not want their followers to visit the Buddha. Thus Upāli, a devotee of Nigaṇṭha Nāthaputta (Jina Mahāvīra) was about to go and see the Buddha to discuss certain religious questions. But the ascetic Dīghatapassi, another disciple of Nigaṇṭha Nāthaputta, advised his master: "Venerable One, do not let your devotee Upāli go near the ascetic Gotama. Gotama is a deceiver. He has a charm which he uses to attract the disciples of other sects" (M I 375; cf. A II 193).

Some more examples will illustrate the spell cast by the Buddha's physical appearance on certain people. Sujātā, the young daughter of a merchant family in the town of Sāketa, happened to see the Buddha on her way home from a carnival. She was so impressed by his gentle and friendly air that she decided there and then to join the Community (Thī 145–150). Kaccāna, one of king Caṇda-Pajjota's ministers, came to take the Buddha to Ujjain. But as soon as he saw him he forgot his mission and decided to renounce lay life (A I 23, Mp 206). Sundara-Samudda, the son of a merchant family in Rājagaha, also decided to become a monk because he was delighted by the Buddha's appearance, (Th 459–465, Th-a I 476). The Buddha's attractiveness also influenced Sigāla-Mātā, a wealthy young woman of Rājagaha; as soon as she had had a child, she asked her husband's permission to renounce family life and join the Community (A I 5, Mp I 342–5). Paripuṇṇaka, from Kapilavatthu, was used to a life of luxury, but decided to renounce lay life when he saw the Buddha's grace and simplicity (Th 91, Th-a I 190). In another story, four friends called Uttiya, Godhika, Subāhu, and Valliya, princes of Malla in the Pāvā country, went to Kapilavatthu on political business. On the way they met the Buddha and decided to leave lay life, abandoning their mission (Th 51–54, Th-a I 133). When the Buddha stayed in Kapilavatthu, a great many young men from the Sākyan families wanted to become monks because they were attracted by his personality (Vin II 180). Prince Nanda, Gotama's cousin, renounced his home, not because he was attracted by the religious life or by the doctrine, but because of the respect which the Buddha inspired in him (Dhp-a I 116). The anecdote of Pukkusāti (M III 237–247) shows that some people renounced lay life in the Buddha's name even without ever having seen or heard him, but on the strength of what they had heard about him, of his reputation.

While some people were directly influenced by the personality of the Buddha, others were influenced by the example of friends or parents. Imitation is a powerful factor, in any society and in regard to all social contexts, particularly in the field of religion. In Buddhist monasticism, some cases of renunciation were motivated solely by a desire to imitate. Let us take some examples. After Yasa's renunciation (Vin I 19), several of his friends decided to follow his example, thinking "this can be no ordinary Doctrine and Discipline, no ordinary renunciation, if Yasa, the son of a good family, has shaven hair and beard, put on the yellow robe and left home for homelessness." The three sisters of Sāriputta Thera, Cālā, Upacālā and Sisupacālā (Thī 182–203, Thī–a 162–168) renounced lay life in imitation of their brother. When the Prince Gotama's foster-mother Mahāpajāpatī Gotamī and his former wife Rāhulamātā became nuns, many women from the Sakyan families decided to follow their example. Amongst them there was the young Abhirūpī-Nandā

(Thī 19–20, Thī–a 168), the greatest beauty in Kapilavatthu. Acording to the *Cullavagga* (Vin II 182), Upāli joined the Community in imitation of his friends Ānanda, Anuruddha, and others. When king Kappina in the kingdom of Kukkuṭavatī renounced lay life, his wives and friends left the palace to go and see the Buddha; they in their turn entered the Community (Mp I 318). If the leader of a religious group accepted the Buddha's teaching, his devotees followed suit. For example, when the great ascetic Uruvela-Kassapa decided to become a disciple of the Buddha, not only his disciples but also his two brothers Gayā-Kassapa and Nadī-Kassapa, along with their disciples, took the same decision (Vin I 32). The desire to follow the example of a leader or of friends could thus lead large numbers of people, whole groups of ascetics or friends, to renounce also. There were exceptions, however. For example, when Sāriputta and Moggallāna decided to become disciples of the Buddha, they were opposed by their teacher Sañjaya of Rājagaha; but they did not heed his advice and went to see the Buddha. Many of Sañjaya's pupils, moreover, followed their example (Vin I 41). After hearing a sermon of the Buddha, the *paribbājaka* Sandaka sent his pupils to the Buddhist monastic community (M I 524). But in another incident, the *paribbājaka* Sakuḷadāyi was not able to enter the Buddhist monkhood because of his followers' objections, even though he wanted to do so (M II 39).

As we have seen, some people renounced lay life under the influence of the Buddha. Many of them did not do so because of problems in their lives, but simply felt the need for an ideal, for a more profound and purer way of life. On the other hand, some people embraced the new Doctrine and joined the Community because of their personal difficulties. They sought to avoid or resolve problems due to distressing physical or mental experiences, painful or disgusting, and difficult to forget. Thus Yasa, whom we have already met, a young man from a very wealthy family in Benares, came to see the Buddha and told him of his aversion to worldly life. This might seem surprising, as he was rich and lived in luxury: gold adorned his sandals, he was married, his father and mother loved him. What was his problem? His story shows that a life of luxury can also bring painful and unpleasant experiences. According to the canonical texts, one night after an evening of drinking and pleasure-seeking he had seen women lying around in his house in shameful positions, and the sight had upset him very much. He had realised the dangers arising from sensual pleasures and had felt a profound disgust for them. One might perhaps interpret his inner development in this way: Yasa was a sensitive young man; at the beginning of the night, sensual pleasure and the pleasant atmosphere created by those around him had awakened his sensibility. But as the night progressed, he had not been able to bear the offensive spectacle, and had left (Vin I 15–16). This story might only be a symbolic legend; but it expresses how some people might have renounced lay life because of unpleasant experiences occurring suddenly in an otherwise happy life. Yasa only regained his composure after meeting the Buddha; soon afterwards, he entered the Community.

Other types of experience could lie at the origin of renunciation. It was, for example, the unbearable grief of Kisā-Gotamī, a young mother from Sāvatthi, at the death of her only child, which led her to renounce lay life (Thī–a 174; Dhp-a 1 270). The princess Ubbirī, wife of King Pasenadi, could not console herself for the death of her daughter Jīvā, on whose tomb she went regularly to shed tears. Her great sadness finally caused her to become a Buddhist nun (Thī 51–52, Thī–a 53–55). Vāseṭṭhī, a young mother from Vesāli, ran away from home after the death of her child, and wandered aimlessly. She roamed the streets, not knowing where to go, until she chanced to meet the Buddha in the town of Mithilā; she listened to his words and decided to enter the Community (Thī 133–138, Thī–a 124). Sāmā, a wealthy lady from Kosambi, felt great despair after the death of a woman friend of hers; she too became a nun (Thī 37–38, Thī–a 44). After several marriages, all of which ended badly because of her husbands' mistreatment, Isidāsī heard a sermon preached by the nun

Jinadattā Therī; thereupon she decided to embrace the religious life (Thī 400–407, Thī–a 260). Muttā, the daughter of a brahmin from Kosala, was also very disappointed with married life, and became a nun after she had obtained her husband's permission (Thī 11, Thī–a 14). Uppalavaṇṇā, the daughter of a businessman from Sāvatthi, was a rare beauty, and several young men wanted to marry her. This became a problem and a source of danger for her, and so she decided to renounce lay life (Thī 109).

A very striking story of this kind is that of Datta, "The Buddhist Oedipus." Before Datta's birth, his mother had been thrown out of her house in her husband's absence by her mother-in-law, and the child was born in a travelers' hostel. The young mother joined a traveling caravan and went in search of her husband. But the caravan leader stole the child, and the mother was carried off by a highway robber, by whom she had a daughter. One day she had an argument with her daughter and hit her on the head, causing a wound; filled with fear, she ran off and took refuge in the town of Rājagaha. There she became a courtesan, and the mistress of the rich Datta, not knowing that he was her son. Some time later, Datta married the highway robber's daughter, not realizing she was his half sister. One day, Datta's mistress was arranging the young wife's hair; she saw the wound on her head and asked where she came from. The young woman told her story and was recognised by her mother, who also discovered that Datta was none other than her own son. The two women left Datta in horror and entered the order of nuns. Datta, equally filled with disgust, immediately went to see the Buddha and joined the Community. He led a contemplative life in the forest for two years, and became an Arahant known as Gaṅgātīriya Thera. (Th 127, Th-a II 8; Thī 224, Thī-a 195)

These stories show that some people renounced the world because of problems in their lives. But one cannot deduce that they did not understand the value of the Doctrine and of detachment from the fact that they seemed motivated only by the desire to escape from their troubles. What value did renunciation of this kind possess? Was it serious and rational? Did Buddhist monasticism encourage people to run away from their difficulties? People always try, one way or another, to avoid unhappiness and to find happiness. Buddhist monasticism recognized the existence of problems, but its strategy for inner development did not consist in seeking an immediate solution for those everyday worries; rather, it tried to remove their causes. It explained them from a different point of view; it did suggest ways to avoid small everyday troubles, but as a means of working toward eliminating the root causes of all problems. According to Buddhist monasticism, renunciation was not an escape, but the first of a series of actions aimed at eliminating the real causes of the problems of life and of "the round of rebirth" (*saṃsāra*). For this reason, life in the Community did not constitute an easy way out, as we will try to show throughout the following chapters.

It appears then, that renunciation could be either negatively or positively motivated. But Buddhist monasticism accorded no importance to this distinction: it took into account not the reason why a person renounced, but what that person did after leaving lay life. Moreover, it must be noted that some people joined the Community without having had first to renounce luxury or a good position in life. Sunīta, for example, was a road-sweeper, obviously very poor and of very low caste according to the Brahmanical caste system. The Buddha wanted him to join the Community, and so went up to him in the street. At his approach, Sunīta hid next to a wall, as a sign of respect for the Buddha. The Buddha approached him and asked if he wanted to join the Community. He assented, and later became an Arahant (Th 620–631, Th-a I 540). Pilotika was a poor, lone brahmin in the town of Rājagaha. On the Buddha's advice, the venerable Ānanda admitted him to the community, where he was able to lead a proper religious life (Dhp-a III 84). Poṭṭhapāda was the son of a family of fishermen, but he had refused to become a fisherman himself, and was driven away from home. He became very poor, and went several days without food.

Then the venerable Ānanda gave him some food, taught him the Doctrine, and admitted him to the Community (Pv-a 178–9). A young girl from a brahmin family called Candā, had lost everything when her parents died in an epidemic, and found herself out on the street. One day, when the venerable nun Paṭācārā was eating her meal, Candā came up to her. The nun gave her some food, taught her the Doctrine and had her join the Community, where, after practicing the methods of inner progress, she became an Arahant (Thī 122–126, Thī–a 120). These people were not in a very good social or economic position, and had no reason to miss life in the world. But for Buddhist monasticism this aspect of their renunciation was not important. What mattered was the way in which the "renouncer" led the religious life after joining the Community. So as to understand this attitude better, let us turn our attention to some examples of novice members of the Community.

When people asked to be admitted to the Community, the Buddha and the monks let them join. But they did not always wait for people who already possessed a good understanding of the religious life and the Teaching to come and ask for ordination or admission. They sometimes had very young people join as novices. Such was the case, for example, of Culla-Panthaka (Dhp-a IV 180), Dabbamallaputta (Vin II 74; Dhp-a III 321), Mānava and Sānu (Th-a I 113; Dhp-a IV 18). Sopāka, a little boy who had lost his father, was mistreated by his uncle, who finally abandoned him in a cemetery. The Buddha brought the child to the monastery and had him join the Community as a novice (Th 480, Th-a I 477; Dhp-a IV 176). Kumāra-Kassapa also was very young when he entered the Community as a novice (Dhp-a III 147; Th-a I 332; Ja I 147). The Buddha brought his son Prince Rāhula to the Monastery, where the venerable Sāriputta admitted him as a novice (Vin I 83; Dhp-a I 98). His grandfather Suddhodhana Sākya was saddened by his entry into the religious life. He came to see the Buddha and said "Blessed One, when the Blessed One renounced the world, I felt great unhappiness; and so also did I when Nanda did the same; my unhappiness became extreme when Rāhula followed them. The love of a father for his son, Blessed One, pierces the skin; after piercing the skin it pierces the flesh; after piercing the flesh it pierces the muscles; after piercing the muscles it pierces the bones; after piercing the bones it reaches the marrow and lodges there. I beg of you, Blessed One: it is not right that the venerable monks should confer Ordination on a son without the permission of his father and mother" (Vin I 83).

There was, then, a tendency to have young people enter the religious life well before they were adult. The Buddha had observed that renunciation is difficult once one has settled down to a comfortable worldly life (cf. M I 447–456). Sometimes people wanted to renounce, but could not do so because of their spouse or children. The only way to solve this problem was to allow or make young people enter the Community well before they had grown accustomed to life in the world. Moreover, youth was regarded as the best age at which the learn the pure conduct required of novices. At such a young age, novices had no clear idea of the aim of renunciation. They had simply imitated certain adults, or else obeyed their preceptors. How are we to understand this aspect of Buddhist monasticism? Not only, as we saw earlier, does Buddhism accord little importance to the motive for renunciation, but still more, it does not consider "renunciation" in itself to be essential. From a Buddhist point of view, it matters little whether the candidate has given up anything or not, or has sacrificed anything or not; the essential thing is to enter the religious life. In other words, Buddhist monks and nuns began the Discipline (*vinaya*) and the life of purity (*brahmacariya*) not when they left home, but at the moment when they embarked on religious life in the Community.

For this reason, the Pali texts use the word *pabbajjā* (Sanskrit *pravrajyā*) to denote admission into the Community. The literal meaning of the term is "to leave" or "to leave home"; but in Theravādin terminology, it denotes admission into the Community as a novice, or "Minor Ordination." According to Buddhism, the true act of leaving home (*pabbajjā*) takes place at the time of Minor Ordination into the Community. For example, the ordination of the Five Ascetics is designated in the canonical texts by the term *pabbajjā;* but it is obvious that they had left their homes a long time before their *pabbajjā* into the Community.[2]

Monastic life was an education and a training in the life of purity, leading to the state of Arahantship. All the rules of the Community were regarded as "Educational Precepts" (*sikkhāpadāni*). In order to enter the Community it was not essential to understand in depth the aim of religious life: children who go to school do not understand the aim of the education they receive. A story found in the *Milinda-pañha* illustrates this. A young Brahmin boy called Nāgasena entered the Community as a novice under the influence of venerable Rohana Thera; the latter had admitted him into the community even though he was very young and had not the slightest knowledge either of worldly life or of the aim of monasticism. Later, King Milinda (Menander) asked him (Mil 31–32): "Venerable one, why did you enter the religious life? For what reason and to what end?" The venerable Nāgasena explained that the aim of religious life in the Buddhist Community is to obtain liberation from *dukkha* (suffering) and to attain *nibbāna.* The king asked if he had known this when he entered as a novice. Nāgasena explained: "I did not know why I was entering the Community, nor did I have any idea what the aim was. But I thought at the time, "These monks, the sons of the Sākyans, are learned men; they will give me an education." And so I received that education and now I know the aim of the religious life."

It might seem as if anyone could join the Community for whatever reason. Many anecdotes from the *Vinaya* texts show this was not the case. Let us take only three examples. During a war on the border of the Magadha country several generals who did not want to enter the field of battle joined the Community. At the behest of King Bimbisāra, the Buddha forbade monks to admit soldiers into the Community (Vin I 73–74). Another time, a thief who had escaped from prison joined the Community. There was a popular outcry, and the Buddha forbade monks to admit escaped convicts

(Vin I 75). Lastly, a man who was heavily in debt entered the Community; this provoked sharp criticism from people. The Buddha then forbade monks to admit debtors (Vin I 76).

If Buddhist monasticism does not consider the motive for renunciation, if it concentrates only on the practices followed in the Community, why then did it forbid entry to such individuals? There are three possible explanations. First, the Community was not a place for people to hide, to evade punishment or lead an easy life. Second, if people act in such a way, they are not being honest with themselves. But without honesty it is not possible to practice the life of purity; honesty is one of the main principles of Buddhist monasticism. Finally, to admit deserters, escaped convicts or debtors presented a problem for lay supporters of the Community.

Canonical texts often praise the qualities of the Buddha's "religious" disciples:

> The Community of disciples (*sāvaka-saṅgha*) of the Blessed One behaves rightly, . . . behaves correctly . . . behaves properly. These are the four pairs of beings, the eight beings.[3] Such is the Community of disciples of the Blessed One, worthy of offerings, worthy of hospitality, worthy of gifts, worthy of respect, the greatest field of merit[4] for the world
> (D III 227; M I 37; A I 222; Sii 69, etc.).

This passage clearly refers to those disciples who have attained the higher degrees of inner progress. But many monks and nuns were still quite ordinary people. One did not automatically become an Arahant simply because one had renounced the world or entered the Community; that was only the first step on the path of renunciation. The need for detachment was continuous throughout the religious life, until the attainment of the goal: the state of Arahantship.

Endnotes

1. [The French word *religieux* can be used, as was once common with the English word "religious," to denote those who have

taken monastic vows and who are members of a monastic order. In this book, the word is sometimes used specifically of Buddhist monks and nuns, sometimes more generally of the wider class of world-renouncers or wandering religious mendicants, which includes Jaina monks and nuns and many different Brahmanical and non-Brahmanical ascetics. We translate it according to context.]

2. [See Chapter 7 for the distinction between Minor and Major Ordinations (*pabbajjā, upasampadā*).]
3. [The "four" and "eight beings" refer to disciples at different stages of attainment on the Path. See Glossary under *sotāpanna*, etc; and cf. Appendix 1 pp.158–60 and 2 p.172.]
4. [Good deeds, especially supporting the monastic Community, are regarded as bringing "merit," which will result in good fortune in the future, usually in future rebirths.]

Chapter 2

Dwelling places

Under no circumstances is a monk to reserve for himself a dwelling-place. Anyone who does this breaks the Monastic Rule
(Vin II 166, IV 41)

At first, the Buddha and his disciples had no fixed abode, and never stayed long in the same place. The *Nikāya* texts and the anecdotes found in the *Vinaya* show us how the Buddha traveled around the central region of North India, often with a large group of disciples, but sometimes with only a few, or just one, such as the venerable Ānanda, and sometimes alone. He traveled during the day, and at night he received lodging in the potter's hut, as in Rājagaha (M III 237) or in the town meeting hall. (These places were, it seems, open to monks, nuns, and other ascetics to pass the night on their travels.) When the Buddha first came to Kapilavatthu, Mahānāma-Sākya went to look for a resting-place for him; it turned out to be the newly-built town meeting hall, which he then inaugurated at the request of the Sākyans (M I 353, S IV 182). Before that he had stayed for a few days in ascetics' hermitages, such as that of Bharaṇḍu Kālāma at Kapilavatthu. The canonical texts also mention the names of several forests in which the Buddha stayed. There were also public parks, such as Ambalaṭṭhika in Rājagaha, which were popular resting-places for wandering ascetics. When he stayed in such a place the Buddha had the opportunity to meet and speak with ascetics of other religious traditions. Naturally his monastic disciples followed the example of the "Great Traveler." They also traveled around, either with their Master or with renowned monks such as Sāriputta or Moggallāna, alone or in groups. Why did the Buddha and his followers travel in this way?

At the time of the Buddha there were many groups of wandering ascetics. Outside the rainy season, Paribbājakas, Ājīvikas, Nigaṇṭhas (Jains) and individual ascetics were constantly on the move; for them traveling was a way to practise detachment. This was not the case, however, for the Buddha and his first disciples: the canonical texts report that they began to travel after they were "liberated from all ties, human and divine." Only a few months after his Enlightenment, before going to the village of Senāni, the Buddha told his little group: "Monks, take to the road: travel for the good of the many; travel for the happiness of the many, out of compassion for the world; travel for the good, benefit and happiness of men and gods. Preach the Doctrine" (Vin I 20–21). This advice, or rather this command, clearly shows why and to what end they traveled. They went out to take a religious message to society, "for the good of the many." There were then only sixty disciples, and the Buddha sent them all over the country to spread the Doctrine. This wandering life on the road was a good way to advertise the young Master and his Doctrine. His traveling disciples attracted people to the new religious movement through their appearance, their good conduct, and the sermons in which they set forth the Master's teaching. Every day, so the Vinaya texts tell us, these monks admitted many new members into the Community.

Thus at first, it was the intention to spread the Doctrine which made traveling necessary. In the course of time, the monks and nuns who took part in these journeys came to include not only those who had attained the higher stages of inner progress, but also those who had not. Some of them in Rājagaha travelled throughout the year, even during the rainy season. People criticized them, according to the *Mahavagga* (Vin I 137):

> At that time the Blessed One had not yet imposed on the monks the rule regarding the Rainy Season Retreat; the monks traveled both during the summer and during the rainy season. People were annoyed, and complained angrily: "How is it that these ascetics, the sons of the Sākyans, keep on traveling during the summer, winter and also in the rainy season? They tread on young plants and damage them, and destroy many small living creatures. Those who belong to other schools may not be very well-disciplined, but at least they withdraw somewhere to make a residence for the rainy season; birds make their nests in the tree-tops and use them to live in during the rainy season: but these ascetics, the sons of the Sākyans, don't stop traveling during the summer, winter and the rainy season as well." Some monks told the Buddha that people were annoyed and had made angry complaints. As a result of this, the Blessed One preached a sermon to the monks and decreed: "Monks, you should observe a retreat during the rainy season."

The idea was not only to provide shelter for the monks, but also to forbid travel throughout the rainy season. According to the *Mahāvagga* the rule was: "A monk observing the Rainy Season Retreat must not travel before he has completed the retreat." The rainy season lasted four months, roughly from June to October. Each monk had to observe the retreat for three months, at the beginning or end of that time.

From then on all monks were obliged to stay for those three months in one place, but they were not allowed to settle just anywhere. They were specifically forbidden to observe the retreat in the open air, in a hollow tree, in a graveyard, under an umbrella, or in an earthenware salt-jar. (According to the *Mahāvagga* (Vin I 152) such places were sometimes used by ascetics at that time as shelter for the rainy season.) Other forms of shelter were allowed by the rules. For example, a monk could spend the retreat in a boat, or with a merchant-caravan: this shows that in some circumstances monks were allowed to travel with lay followers during the rainy season. For the most part, monks observed the retreat in cells that they or lay-followers had built. Each cell housed one or two monks; these shelters were temporary structures, erected in a forest, next to a river, in a valley or at the foot of a mountain, but always close to a village or town.

At the end of the Rainy Season Retreat the monks would take down their cells and resume traveling, although some monks, apparently, would have liked to stay put even after the retreat (see Vin I 152). The monk Dhaniya, for example, did not take down his beautiful cell, but wanted to live in it during the summer. The Buddha and his fellow-monks disapproved of his intention, and he was obliged to abandon it. As a result of this incident rules were laid down forbidding monks and nuns to remain without traveling after the retreat (Vin III 42). So although the life of Buddhist monks was a nomadic one, in the course of their travels they also had periods of sedentary life. But how was this sedentariness introduced into the monks' wandering life? There are two possible explanations: first, the custom of staying in a fixed abode during the rainy season, and second the increase in the number of lay-followers, concerned for the well-being of these "renouncers."

Some scholars think that the institution of the Rainy Season Retreat served as a bridge between two different periods in the history of the Buddhist monastic Community: first wandering and then sedentary life. But I do not think that we are dealing here with a transformation, or with two different stages. The institution of the Retreat served rather to connect two different styles of life: traveling and being settled in one place. The *Vinaya Piṭaka* and the *Sutta Piṭaka* show that even after being given places to live, the Master and his disciples did not abandon traveling. We will return to this point.

"Traveling" for a monk did not mean walking constantly day and night. When a group of monks arrived in a town or a village they might stay for several days or weeks, for as long as there were people to listen to the Buddha's teaching. Sometimes monks would come to the town where the Master was staying to visit him, and spend some time with him. Sometimes the Buddha and his monks would stay for a few days in an ascetic's hermitage or in a public place in the town; even outside the rainy season they had to find a quiet place to spend the night. We know that several parks were set aside for the Buddha and his disciples by lay-followers. According to the *Mahāvagga,* the first park of this kind was given by King Bimbisāra, a friend and lay disciple of the Buddha, only a few weeks after his Enlightenment. The *Mahāvagga* (Vin I 38) gives the following account of the event: "the king of Magadha, Seniya Bimbisāra, took a ceremonial golden cup filled with water, poured it over the Blessed One's hand,[1] and thus made the donation: 'Blessed One, I give this Bamboo Grove to the Community with the Blessed One at its head'; then the Blessed One accepted the park."

Thus from the beginning the new Community owned some grounds. Nevertheless, monks still did not make a practice of building shelters, or of having them built, to live in outside the rainy season; nor indeed were they allowed to do so. The Cullavagga (Vin II 146) gives us the following account of the first occasion on which the Community accepted lodgings. It took place at Rājagaha:

> At that time lodgings had not been permitted to the monks by the Blessed One. So the monks stayed here and there, in a forest, at the foot of a tree. . . in a mountain cave, a cemetery, a forest glade, in the open air, on a heap of straw. They left these places early in the morning. . . One day a great merchant from Rājagaha wanted to have residences built for the monks. He asked them, "Venerable Sirs, if I have lodgings built for you, will you be able to live in them?" The monks answered "No, householder, lodgings have not been allowed by the Blessed One." The great merchant said to the monks, "Venerable Sirs, ask the Blessed One and tell me what he says." The monks passed on his proposal to the Blessed One, who answered, "Monks, I allow five kinds of dwelling-places: an ordinary residence (*vihāra*), residences which are round (*aḍḍhayoga*), long (*pasāda*), or with several stories (*hammiya*), and a cave." On the strength of this permission, the great merchant had several residences built and gave them to the Community.

Soon Anāthapiṇḍika, a great banker from Sāvatthi and one of the most devoted lay disciples, bought a park for the Buddha and his disciples on which he had large dwelling-places built, which included cells, store-rooms, meeting-rooms, rooms with a fire-place, places to store gifts, toilets, meditations walk-ways, rooms next to wells,[2] rooms for hot baths, and lotus ponds. He then gave this large monastery to the community. On the road from Rājagaha to the town of Sāvatthi where the Buddha had come to accept the donation from Anāthapiṇḍika, people built many monasteries for the Community. The Buddha made the journey between the two cities (a distance of around 200 miles) several times (Vin II 158–159).

The *Gaṇaka Moggallāna-sutta* (M III 1. cf. S V 269–270) mentions the fact that the monastery in Sāvatthi, whose construction was financed by Visākhā-Migāra-Mātā, was a seven-story building; it took many years to complete. The great monastery known as Kukkuṭārāma in Kosambi was built by a banker called Kukkuṭa. He also built several monasteries on the road from Sāvatthi to Kosambi for the Buddha and his disciples to rest while traveling between the two towns. Lamotte calculates that the Community owned twenty-nine large monasteries at that time: eighteen in Rājagaha, four in Vesāli, three in Sāvatthi, and four in Kosambi.[3] One can easily imagine that there must have been many more monasteries, large and small, in every region where monks were expected to travel and to stay.

We should notice the particular atmosphere of these monasteries: King Bimbisāra who gave the park in Rājagaha and Anāthapiṇḍika who had a monastery built in Sāvatthi are said to have thought, "Where indeed can the Blessed One dwell? He needs a place which is not too close to a town, but not too far either, where people can come and go, easy of access for those who wish to visit, not crowded during the day, peaceful at night, a place away from people, sheltered from disturbances and crowds, and appropriate for the religious life" (Vin I 38–39, II 158). This story shows that lay followers had definite ideas about what kinds of residence were fit for the Community. Buddhist monasteries were built neither too close to a town or village, nor too far away. Lay followers could go there to visit the Buddha and his disciples. People who approved of the new Doctrine and of the behavior of the Community began to build them places to live. The *Cullavagga* mentions a rapid increase in the number of residences built from the time the rule allowed monks to accept them. From then on, rules would be required to regulate these matters.

Rules about Dwelling-Places

Most of these rules were established with two intentions in mind: monks should not stray from a simple way of life, and they should not abuse the generosity of their benefactors. Some monks wanted to build cells or larger residences, with the help of lay donors. But the Buddha forbade them to do so in whatever manner and wherever they pleased. Monks had to limit the size of the residences they built, and the building site had to be approved by the Community. If a benefactor, on the other hand, had a monastery built, or added some rooms to a monastery, he could do so without regard for size, but the building site still had to be approved by the Community. The construction of a residence was not to entail the destruction of plant life or of ancient sanctuaries belonging to other religions, and there had to be an open space around the building. Once the building work was completed, monks were not allowed to importune the benefactor with requests for more rooms. These rules were intended to avoid making difficulties for the donor, and to encourage monks to keep to a simple way of life (*Saṅghādisesa* rules 6–7, Vin III 144–157).

Rules about Furniture

Monks and nuns were allowed to use the kind of furniture found in households at that time. According to the *Cullavag-*

ga (Vin II 150, IV 39), they had a choice of four kinds of beds and five kinds of mattresses to sleep on: a long bed, a bed with slats, with curved legs, or with removable legs. Even a canopy was permitted. The five kinds of mattresses were those made of wool, of cotton, of bark, of tiṇa-grass, and of leaves. Monks and nuns could make use of chairs, stools and small sitting mats. Carpets also were allowed, but they had to be made of cotton (Vin II 150).

As the number of followers increased, monasteries were given a lot of furniture. Some over-generous lay people chose to give the Community furniture and other things which did not fit in with the reqirement of a simple way of life. When some monks made use of these objects, people started to criticize them, in the following words: "Look at these monks, sons of the Sākyans, living in luxury like lay people!" The criticisms came to the Buddha's ears: he forbade members of the Community to use certain things in the monasteries, such as large cushions, divans, bedspreads of thick fur, woollen bedspreads printed with flowers, cotton bedspreads printed with animal figures, bedside rugs, carpets brocaded with gold or silk, thick woollen carpets, deer or leopard skins, beds with a canopy or decked with crimson cushions on one or both sides, and so forth (Vin I 192). When King Pasenadi Kosala's grandmother died, the king gave her furniture to the Community, but these royal pieces did not conform to the rule. On the Buddha's advice, the monks made use of the royal sofas after cutting the legs short, and of the divans after removing the horsehair mattresses (Vin II 169). Monks were forbidden to use large beds or chairs with legs over eight inches high (*Pācittiya* rule 87, nuns' *Pācittiya* 163); if they were higher, they had to be cut down (Vin IV 167). Of the ten precepts applicable to novices, the ninth enjoined abstinence from the use of seats and beds which were wide and luxurious (Vin I 83–84).[4]

Here we have to ask: who owned all these goods? Had Buddhist monks become members of the property-owning class because they were given plots of land, buildings, furniture, and other material possessions? One might think that the Buddha and his disciples had renounced everything and embraced the religious life, only to start living in a new house called "a monastery." However, a closer look at their life shows that there is no contradiction between renunciation and accepting parks, monasteries and furniture. Monasteries and furniture were not the private property of Buddhist monks and nuns. According to the *Vinaya* texts, King Bimbisāra made his gift of a royal park to "the Community which has the Buddha at its head," as did the great banker of Rājagaha who had residences built for the monks. Jetavana, a monastery in Sāvatthi, was also donated to "the Community which has the Buddha at its head." Every example to be found in the texts shows that donations were not personal gifts. To express the idea of gifts to "the Community which has the Buddha at its head," Pali texts and donative inscriptions use a special phrase: "the Community of monks from the four corners of the world, present and absent, which has the Buddha at its head" (*buddhapamukkha āgatānāgata cātuddisa saṅgha*) (Vin I 305, II, 147). (See Chapter 1, p. 1.) In this way benefactors always donated gifts to the Community without mention of particular persons (cf. M III 253–257).

In the first years, there were no rules concerning common ownership and common use. Things were simple and clearcut among the first disciples. They would come to a monastery, stay there, and then leave without any problem. Later on, however, it is said that as the number of members of the Community increased, some bogus "renouncers" among them tried to take possession of residences for themselves. As a result, a rule was established: "Under no circumstances is a monk to reserve for himself a dwelling place. Anyone who does this breaks the Monastic Rule" (Vin II 165, IV 41). Furthermore, in order to prevent this kind of situation from arising again, the Community entrusted to a responsible monk the task of allocating lodgings. When monks arrived at a monastery, he was the one to assign them a place to stay (Vin II 75, IV 291). He was not to be accused of partiality or favoritism (Vin IV 43).

When a monk arrived in a monastery, he had to behave so as not to disturb sick or aged monks (*Pācittiya* rule 16, Vin IV

41–42, nuns' *Pācittiya* 112). No monk or nun had the right to throw another out of the monastery (*Pācittiya* rule 17, nuns *Pācittiya* 35). No monks or nuns were allowed to reserve a place for themselves in two monasteries (Vin II 207). When monks and nuns arrived in a monastery, they had to be received with the greatest courtesy; rules concerning the proper welcome are clearly defined in the *Cullavagga* (Vin II 208–210). The newcomers also had to show due respect. They were free to stay in any place belonging to the Community, as long as there was room. They had the right to make use of the furniture, but were required to do so with care, as it was common property. Before leaving, they had to put everything back in its place (*Pācittiya* rule 14, Vin IV 38–39, nuns' *Pācittiya* 110); they were not, for example, to leave pieces of furniture outside in the open, but had to put them back inside the monastery. If they could not tidy up themselves, they had to get someone else to do so. Before leaving, they had to leave everything clean and tidy (*Pācittiya* rule 15, Vin IV 40, nuns' *Pācittiya* 111). When a nun left a residence, she had to entrust it to the care of another nun. Nuns were not allowed to leave their residence, even to go begging, without making some such arrangement (*Pācittiya* rule 48 from the *Bhikkhunī-vibhaṅga*, Vin IV 303).

Objects belonging to the Community could never become the private property of any individual person. *Pācittiya* rules 82 and 160 forbid monks and nuns respectively to distribute or to transfer common property (Vin IV 155). The regulations laid down in the *Cullavagga* (Vin II 169) show precisely the attitude of the Community toward common property in detail:

> There are five things, monks, which may not be transferred or distributed by the Community, nor by a group of two or three monks, nor by a monk alone. What are they? A monastery or building site for a monastery is the first thing which may not be transferred or distributed by the Community, nor by a group of two or three monks, nor by a monk alone. If it were distributed or transferred, the transaction would not be

> valid. The monks responsible for it would have committed a serious offence. A residence or building site for a residence is the second . . . (as above) . . . A bed, a chair or a mattress is the third. . . A large copper vase, a copper jar, a copper pot, a razor, an axe, a hatchet or a hoe is the fourth. . . Creepers, bamboos, muñja and babbaja grass, tiṇa-grass,[5] clay, wooden or earthenware objects are the fifth. . .

So not only were the monasteries and furniture considered common property, but also tools and artifacts, and plants growing on the monastery grounds. Monks did not have the right to own them in person, to accept them as their own or to distribute them. No person or group had the authority to change or to debate the absolute character of this rule. In other words, even with the unanimous agreement of the Community, the above-mentioned goods were not to be given away or distributed. These rules give us quite a clear picture of the living conditions of the Buddhist "renouncers," and of their attitude toward material objects, especially their residences. One important question remains: did the monks give up their travelling once they had the possibility to settle down in one place?

Traveling as Part of a Settled Way of Life

We have said that in the early days, Buddhist monks traveled not because it was a virtue in itself, but in order to spread the Doctrine, on the advice of their Master. Thus residences and monasteries gave them no reason to neglect the obligation to travel. Every speech by the Buddha, every discussion between the disciples in the *Sutta piṭaka,* and every episode in the *Vinaya piṭaka,* show that the Master and his disciples still traveled from place to place, even though they had monasteries at their disposal. In fact, these monasteries made their wandering easier: if they were tired or it was evening, monks could take shelter in the nearest monastery. The

Cullavagga (Vin II 75) depicts monks arriving in Rājagaha very late at night, and the monk in charge of allocating lodgings ready to welcome them and see to their needs. In the normal course of things, every residence and every monastery would be occupied by monks and nuns during the rainy season. After the Retreat, they would be on their way. Some would go and visit the Buddha (see Vin I 158, 253), to ask his advice, to learn meditation practices, to listen to new teachings, or to have him answer questions concerning the Doctrine or the Discipline. Novices would accompany their preceptors, since traveling was no obstacle to their training. Pupils whose preceptors lived and preached the Doctrine in distant places also wanted to meet the Buddha. The young monk called Soṇa-Kuṭikanna for example, a pupil of the well-known Mahā-Kaccāna Thera, is said to have thought, "It is true that I have heard about the Buddha, that he is like this, or like that; but I have never met him face to face. I want to go and see him, if my preceptor will let me." He was granted permission and entrusted with an important message from his preceptor, and went from Avanti to Sāvatthi to see the Buddha (Vin I 195).[6]

After the rainy season, the Master too would have to travel with a large or small group of monks. Sometimes he would journey from one monastery to another to visit his disciples (Vin I 294). When the Buddha and his group traveled a long way, they could rest in residences close to their route. In that way, monasteries had become part of the Community's travelling lifestyle. At the same time, they became centers for lay disciples in the locality.

Another piece of evidence for the fact that monks continued to travel after they had been given monasteries is found in the traditional formula used by lay followers when they donated residences or monasteries to the monks: "To the monks from the four corners of the world, present and absent, who have the Buddha at their head." This clearly shows that monks traveled even after they were given monasteries, and that every monastery was open to every monk in the Community. A commentarial text (Mp IV 186) says that even a small leaf-hut qualifies as a monastery built for "monks from the four corners of the world" on the following conditions: it contains a *stūpa,* the Doctrine is preached there, monks come there "from the four corners of the world," wash their feet and open the door with the key, set up beds, spend some time there and leave when they wish.

It is not true to say, however, that monasteries were completely empty most of the time, apart from when visiting monks came to stay: they also housed monks who were permanent residents. When sick or old, a monk was not under the obligation to travel and was allowed to stay in one place for as long as he wanted. Monks with specific functions in the Community, the ones in charge of allocating lodgings for example, also had the right to settle down permanently in a monastery. On the other hand, if someone was neither sick nor old, he was not encouraged to remain without traveling (A III 258). At the end of the Rainy Season Retreat, even nuns had to leave their residences; moreover, they had to travel a certain distance (*Pācittiya* rule 40 from the *Bhikkhunī-vibhaṅga,* Vin IV 296). To regulate nuns' travel, several rules were laid down in the *Pātimokkha:* for example, *Pācittiya* rules 37, 38, 39 and 40 (Vin IV 294–295) dealt with how and where they could travel.

Thus, it is clear that even when they had monasteries, monks still did not have permanent accommodation, as they did not give up their obligation to travel. The arrangements for the Community's dwelling-places, and especially the fact of their common ownership, were designed to avoid conflict with the ideal of non-attachment.

Endnotes

1. This is a sign that something is being donated to someone. The Chronicles of Ceylon tell us that during the ceremony of the donation of Mahāmeghavana to the Community, King Devānampiyatissa (307–267 B.C.) poured water from a golden cup onto the hands of the Venerable Mahinda (Mhv Chap. 15,

vv. 14–15, 24–25). Still today in Sri Lanka when Buddhists give a monastery or ground for a monastery to the Community, they observe this custom.

2. The monks drew water from these wells to take baths, and they could keep their robes in these "rooms next to wells," which were small huts built alongside.
3. Lamotte (88) pp.17ff.
4. [For the Ten Precepts taken by novices, see Appendix 3.]
5. These creepers and grasses were used for ropes, basketwork, mattresses, and other things.
6. [The content of this message is described in Chapter 3, pp. 53–4.]

Chapter 3

Clothing

> *Just as a bird takes its wings with it wherever it flies, so the monk takes his robes and his begging-bowl with him wherever he goes; he is content with robes for his body and a begging-bowl for his stomach. . .*
>
> (D I 71; M III 35; A II 209)

The clothes worn by monks and nuns are one of the most important symbols of the religious life. A frequent passage in the *Nikāya* texts tells us what was worn by those who had renounced life in the world: "I wish to have my hair and beard cut, wear *kāsāya* robes and leave my family, going from home to homelessness." The phrase *kāsāyavatthāni* refers to the usual dress of renouncers at the time of the Buddha; but it is not clear immediately what it means: the Pali adjective *kāsāya* denotes the color yellow or ochre, and the term *vatthāni* denotes materials, clothes or robes. What were these ochre-colored materials or robes? What were their dimensions? The texts do not say. The color ochre was probably the only specific trait common to the robes of ascetics at the time of the Buddha.

Many passages from the *Vinaya* show that there was a well-defined way of dressing in Buddhist monasticism. In fact, rules on this subject were much more numerous that rules about lodgings and food. In the *Pātimokkha,* 19 *Nissaggiya Pācittiya* rules and 7 *Pācittiya* rules deal with clothing. In the *Mahāvagga,* three chapters are devoted to specific details about clothing. These rules seem to have been established at a definite stage in the evolution of the Community: according to the *Vinaya*, they date from about twenty years after the Buddha's Enlightenment. According to the *Mahāvagga*, during the first twenty years the Buddha and his disciples wore a robe called *paṃsukūla cīvara* (Vin I 289), a garment made of rags. In other religious systems, some ascetics wore garments made of grass or of tree bark, others were clothed in hair, in owl feathers, or deer skins (Vin I 305). Yet others, for example the Nigaṇṭhā, disciples of Jina Mahāvīra and the Acelakā, remained completely naked (Vin I 282). The members of the Buddhist Community, however, and its founder, were not willing to acknowledge nudity as a virtue, nor to imitate the mode of dress of any other ascetics. This is why they adopted a costume made up of rags that they had collected. The *Mahāvagga* does not explain the size of this robe nor how many pieces it was made of.

According to the *Vinaya*, two kinds of rag were used to make up the garments of Buddhist monks. Some were pieces of cloth collected in burial-grounds, others were scraps of material gathered in streets and near shops. We do not know where the first kind came from; perhaps they were the clothes corpses had been dressed in, or perhaps people threw them away in cremation-grounds specifically for ascetics to gather. The *Vinaya* describes how traveling monks, in the first years of the Community, would collect rags in cremation-grounds which they chanced to find on their way. It is possible that people deliberately threw pieces of material there for that purpose. However, the fact that monks used rags gathered in cremation-grounds did not mean that they wore dirty garments, or saw a special virtue in doing so. On the contrary, the *Vinaya* describes them washing the rags before using them. We do not know the origin of the pieces of cloth that monks collected in streets and in front of shops either. Perhaps they were old and worn out, perhaps they were thrown away on purpose for the monks to use. In any case, Buddhist monks wore garments made of rags; this kind of costume probably constituted a simple and economical solution. For lodgings and food monks relied on lay followers, but they do not seem to have asked them for clothes directly.

Twenty years after the beginning of the Community, an incident occurred which made it possible for monks to accept the robes and pieces of cloth given to them by lay people, as is described in the *Mahāvagga* (Vin I 280):

> In those days, every monk would wear rag-robes. One day when the Blessed One was in Rājagaha, he fell ill. He was examined by the royal doctor, called Jīvaka-Komārabacca,[1] and recovered thanks to the medicine that he prescribed. Soon afterwards, Jīvaka came back to visit him, bringing a piece of costly fabric which he wished to give to the Buddha, and told him: "Blessed One, you wear only a rag-robe and the Community follows your example. Now, Blessed One, this fabric called Sīveyyaka[2] which I was given by King Pajjota is of the highest quality. I beg you, Blessed One, to accept these two pieces of fabric to make a robe for yourself. I also beg you to allow the Community to accept pieces of material given by lay people." The Buddha accepted the fabric given by the royal doctor, and on this occasion addressed the monks in the following words: "Monks, I allow you to accept pieces of material given by lay people, and to wear the robes made from them. Monks, I allow you to wear robes given by lay followers, or to continue wearing rag-robes."

Henceforth, the dress of Buddhist monks and nuns began to be governed by rules; before this declaration, according to the *Vinaya,* there were no specific rules about rag-robes.

Did Buddhist monks, in accepting donations from their followers, deviate from the path of renunciation? One might wonder why the Buddha accepted Jīvaka's offer. It was probably in his capacity as a doctor that Jīvaka intervened in the matter of clothing, out of consideration for the physical health of the Buddha and of his disciples. Although the *Vinaya* does not say so, the circumstances in which Jivaka brought the fabric to the Buddha suggest that there was a link between the Buddha's illness and the new robe. Moreover, as the number of monks increased, it probably became difficult to find enough rags for everybody. It was right and proper to allow other ways of obtaining material to make robes. It looks as if the Master was only waiting to be asked by devotees to allow monks to wear robes given by lay people. If the Buddha and his disciples had started from the first days to beg for robes made with unused pieces of material, and to accept them, this would undoubtably have hindered their popularity. Twenty years later, a large enough number of devotees accepted that wearing a robe made up of pieces of material given by lay people was no obstacle on the path of inner progress; and so they asked the Buddha and his disciples to wear the robes they had given them, or to use material they had given. For the Buddha, the time was now ripe to change the habits of the Community and accept unused fabrics to make monastic garments. However, monks did not give up their costume made of rags completely. If he so desired, a monk could still wear rag-robes, but new rules were laid down to specify their precise dimensions and color, following those applying to robes given by lay followers.

As for the general appearance of the robes, some scholars think that at first the dimension and shape of the Buddhist monks' costume were not very different from those of lay people. A monk called Upananda wanted to get one of the pieces of material worn by the son of a great banker in Sāvatthi (Vin III 210). If the clothes of the banker's son had not been similar to those of monks, the argument has it, then Upananda would not have been able to make his request. In my opinion, this anecdote does not offer conclusive proof that the garments worn by monks and by lay people were similar. Upananda did not ask for that piece of material in order to dress in some unusual fashion; he wanted to make a robe fit for a monk with it, following the dimensions and shapes specified in the rules of the *Vinaya*. It is logical to assume that after he permitted monks to accept fabric and robes given by lay followers, the Buddha imposed specific rules for monks' clothes. It is hard to believe that renouncers, used to rag-robes, could have adopted clothes exactly similar to those of lay people.

According to the *Mahāvagga,* the monk's costume comprised three pieces, or rather three robes: one with a lining, to be worn as an outer cloak if need be, and called *saṅghāṭi,* one without a lining, called *uttarāsaṅga,* worn as a toga, and one used as underclothing, the *antarāvāsaka.* The three robes were still symbolically related to the rag-robe: just as rag-robes were made of pieces of cloth sewn together, so also the robes given by lay followers would have to be made of several pieces of cloth sewn together. Buddhist monks were not allowed to wear a robe made from a single, uncut piece of material. So a piece of cloth given by lay followers could not be used immediately; it had to be cut into several pieces following the dimensions specified in the *Vinaya,* and these had then to be sewn together. Only when the original piece of material, whatever its size, had been cut up and sewn according to the prescribed dimensions, did it become a suitable robe. One day the Buddha asked the venerable Ānanda to create a pattern for monk's robes, modeled on a field of rice in Magadha country which was divided into sections by banks of earth. With great care Ānanda prepared a pattern following this model, and the Buddha accepted this robe as suitable for his disciples. In order to make such a robe, it was necessary first to cut up the material into several pieces (Vin I 287).

The three monastic robes were rectangular.[3] So why, one may ask, did monks cut up a new piece of cloth into several smaller ones, to make their robe? Why did they not use a piece of cloth of the right dimensions which they would not have to cut up? The idea was to reduce the original value of the cloth to a minimum: even a very costly piece of material loses its commercial value when it is cut up in small bits. Monks were indeed given valuable fabrics by lay followers: they could not refuse costly pieces of cloth which were not suitable for them, but they could destroy their commercial value before using them. In that way they transformed them into clothes in keeping with the spirit of renunciation; and these clothes were not "suitable for lay people, nor for thieves" (Vin I 209). (On several occasions, however, monks' robes were stolen by enemies of the Community (Vin I 283–298, III 211, IV 119).)

Nuns also wore three robes similar to the monks', with two extra pieces: a vest called *samakaccikā*, and a bathing garment called *udakasāṭikā* (Vin II 272, IV 280–282). Nuns were forbidden to go to a town or village without a vest (*Pācittiya* rule 96 from the *Bhikkhunī-vibhaṅga*, Vin IV 345), to bathe naked (*Pācittiya* rule 21, Vin IV 276; see Vin I 293, II 280), or to wear dirty robes (*Pācittiya rule 47, Vin IV 324).*

According to the *Vinaya* texts and some stories from the *Nikāya*s, the color of ascetics' clothes was usually ochre or yellow. Therefore, the rag-robes worn in the first years of the Community must have been that color; but there is no rule which lays down the correct color for robes in general. Some rules, however, do specify which colors are unsuitable. The *Mahāvagga* (Vin I 306, see Vin II 268) tells of some monks who tried, in the first days of the Community, to wear blue, brown, yellowish brown, pale yellow, dark yellow, crimson or even black robes. As lay followers criticized these colors, the Master forbade monks and nuns to wear them. They were not allowed to wear white either. The *Mahāvagga* (Vin I 281) gives a list of permitted dyes: they were made from roots, tree-bark, leaves, flowers and stalks. One or more of these ingredients would be put in a big pot with boiling water, until the water became the right color. This process of dyeing was also intended to reduce the commercial value of the original piece of cloth.

The Kinds of Fabric Used

Once permission had been given, the Community received different kinds of material from lay people. On this subject, the Buddha was more broad-minded than the other religious leaders of his time. He did not hesitate to accept even costly fabrics. He allowed his disciples to make use of six kinds of material: linen, cotton, silk, wool, coarse linen and hemp (Vin I 281). The first four were regarded, even in the Buddha's time, as valuable, and were given to the Community by wealthy followers (see A IV 394). For the Buddha, the quality of fabric did not represent a major obstacle on the path of renunciation. In any case, monks' robes were not rich garments, since they were made up of several pieces. However, monks were not allowed to incite weavers to make them better, more beautiful pieces of cloth (*Nissaggiya Pācittiya* rule 27, nuns' *Nissaggiya Pācittiya 28*). Monks were only allowed to have cloth woven for them if the weavers were devout followers of the Community or very close members of their own family (Vin III 256–260). Nuns were not allowed to weave fabrics themselves (Pācittiya rule 43 from the *Bhikkhunīvibhaṅga,* Vin IV 299).

The Robe Called "Kaṭhina-cīvara"

The seventh chapter of the *Mahāvagga* is entirely devoted to the description of this robe, or rather of both the robe and the ceremony involving it. They are specifically related to the Rainy Season Retreat. According to the *Mahāvagga* (Vin I 253), they first appeared when a group of monks came from Sāketa to visit the Buddha in Sāvatthi, just after the Rainy Season Retreat. Their robes were dirty, stained, spoiled and threadbare, because they had traveled from Sāketa on muddy roads and sometimes in the rain. The Buddha saw that they needed new robes and decided to allow his disciples to accept a robe or a piece of cloth at the end of the Rainy Season Retreat (the *kaṭhina*). The literal meaning of the Pali term *kaṭhina* is "hard"; according to the *Vinaya* Commentary the robe and the ceremony were called *kaṭhina* because the gift of this robe was an act of merit as hard as a diamond. The phrase *kaṭhina-cīvara* designates the robe given to the Community by lay people at the end of the Rainy Season Retreat. The fabric used to make it was called *kaṭhina-vattha*. Not all the pieces of cloth brought by lay people on that occasion were regarded as *kaṭhina-vattha,* but only those which the Community approved for the robe. To be approved, a fabric had to fulfill the following conditions:

a) It had to be new. Pieces of cloth used to cover over a corpse or left in cremation-grounds or in the streets were unsuitable. However, a robe which had been worn by an individual monk, or a piece of cloth which had been used by a lay person, male or female, could be accepted as *kaṭhina-vattha* if it was undamaged and conformed to the rules.

b) the donor or donors had to make the gift of their own free will: monks were not allowed to obtain the cloth by means of hints or praise, and still less by means of flattery, insinuation or threat.

c) Last, the cloth had to be prepared, by being well cleaned and then stretched out by someone formally appointed to do so by the Community; it had also to be measured, and to have an edge and a proper hem.

Once the cloth was prepared and approved by the Community as *kaṭhina-vattha,* it could be used to make a robe. If the robe was of the correct size and shape, it would be accepted as *kaṭhina-cīvara* by the Community. The dimensions and appearance of the *kaṭhina-cīvara* were not different from those of the other robes, but it was offered to the Community at the end of the Rainy Season Retreat, during a ceremony involving lay followers: they attended the dedication ritual, which provided them with an opportunity to earn merit, and was an important ritual occasion. The monks and nuns taking part in the ceremony represented the Community, and would give such robes to those who had spent the Retreat according to the rules. For monks, the ceremony represented a formal act of the Community; for lay people, it symbolized the culminating point of their hospitality towards the monks during the rainy season.

The Meaning of Monastic Dress

As we mentioned above, in the first days of the Community, the Buddha and his disciples wore robes made up of rags they had collected. Such garments symbolized detachment and the humble way of life adopted by the renouncers of the new Community; when they accepted gifts from laity, they made use of them in the spirit of renunciation. But Buddhist monastic dress did not conform to the notion of detachment held by renouncers of other religious systems. As we have seen, some ascetics wore tree bark or animal skins, others even practiced nakedness as a sign of detachment. As in the matter of food and lodgings, the Buddha did not want to adopt extreme solutions in the matter of dress. He knew from experience that such practices were not conducive to inner progress. Even rag-robes were not a mark of extremism. They were the best and easiest solution to the problem of dress, given the religious context of the time. When the situation changed, the Buddha did not hesitate to adopt a better solution: gifts from lay people.

In order to safeguard the spirit of religious detachment, he forbade monks to decorate or color their robes in several rules found in the *Cullavagga* (Vin II 136). If a monk decorated his robe, by adding gold or silver trimmings, he was guilty of breaking the law. This prohibition insured that their uniform mode of dress put all members of the Community, including novices, on an equal footing. In addition, the Buddha clearly forbade his disciples to take an interest in fashion and indulge in vanity. Neither monks (Vin II 106) nor nuns (Vin IV 338–340) were allowed to wear ornaments. The rules laid down in the *Cullavagga* (Vin II 107) forbade the use of combs, mirrors or ointments to monks, as they shaved their heads completely. Monks and nuns were forbidden ever to let their hair grown longer than two inches. This practice obviously embodied the rejection of all worldly frivolities.

On one hand the Buddha was opposed to ascetic austerities; on the other hand, he rejected fashion and vanity. He forbade monks to accumulate clothes, as this was contrary to the spirit of the religious life: he limited them to three robes. This restriction was necessary as some monks wanted to possess a large number of robes. According to the *Mahāvagga* (Vin I 288), when the Buddha was traveling between

Rājagaha and Vesāli, he saw some of his disciples carrying bundles of robes on their shoulders, and thought to himself: "These stupid men give too much importance to the details of their costume. It would be a good idea if I were to set a limit to the number of robes that a monk may possess." So the Buddha allowed monks three robes out of consideration for their physical well-being, but forbade them any more. If a monk already possessed three, he was not allowed to accept another, unless it was a *kaṭhina* robe. If a monk was given any robes, he was obliged to share them among those whose robes were worn out, or to donate them to the monastery's store. Rules and advice concerning the Buddhist monk's dress expressed and reinforced the spirit of detachment from material values.

The Master valued detachment from material things, but he was also concerned with the physical well-being of his disciples. The dress of Buddhist monks and nuns was in no way a form of penance. In their eyes, clothes were a means to "protect the body against cold, heat, mosquitoes, insects and the wind" (M I 10). Why then did the Buddha think that three robes were necessary to his disciples' physical well-being (four, in a sense, as one of them, the *saṅghāṭi*, was double)? In the following story from the *Mahāvagga* (Vin I 288), he gives these reasons:

> In those days, monks, during the cold winter months, when it rained and snowed, I was in the open air wearing a single robe. I did not feel cold. After the first part of the night, however, I felt cold. I put on a second robe. Then I did not feel cold any more. After the second part of the night, I felt cold again. I put on a third robe. Then I did not feel cold any more. At the end of the night, at sunrise, in the bright light, I felt cold. I put on a fourth robe. Then I did not feel cold any more. At that moment, monks, I thought to myself: "Sons of good family who live according to the Doctrine and the Discipline, who might catch a cold or are afraid of the cold, can all protect themselves with three robes." I allow you, monks, three robes: *saṅghāti, uttarāsaṅga,* and *antarāvāsaka*.

Later on, around ten years before the Buddha's death, Devadatta[4] asked the Master to enact a rule to make rag-robes the obligatory dress for his monks once and for all. The Buddha rejected Devadatta's proposition (Vin II 196), one of the reasons being his concern for his disciples' comfort. Some ascetics of that time regarded lack of comfort as a positive and important value, but the Buddha had rejected extreme asceticism. According to his doctrine of "the middle way," luxury was to be rejected, but a certain level of comfort was deemed necessary. The same attitude is apparent in connection with lodgings and food. If an element of comfort does not become an obstacle to the life of renunciation, Buddhist monasticism does not hold it to be unsuitable for renouncers. On the contrary, in several cases the Buddha indicated that discomfort can actually hinder inner progress. The rules that he decreed on the matter of monastic dress express his concern for the physical well-being of his disciples.

It must be emphasized that the necessity to differentiate Buddhist monks from the ascetics of other religious systems was also a motivation in the choice of such clothes. When the small Community around the Buddha expanded, it became necessary to institute a specific code of conduct for its members, in all areas of life, in order to distinguish them from other ascetics. In this matter, lay followers played an important part. Through their criticism or praise, the benefactors of the Community encouraged monks to behave differently from other renouncers. When they noticed a monk behaving badly, they would say: "there, you see, these monks, sons of the Sākyans, behave just as badly as other ascetics." When, on the contrary, they saw a monk behave rightly, they would say that the monks, sons of the Sākyans, exemplified "right behavior, true behavior, just behavior," etc. Such phrases are repeated in several passages in the *Nikāya* texts as well as in the *Vinaya*.

The Buddha seems to have wanted to maintain a distinction between his disciples' dress and that of other ascetics. One finds an example of this in the *Mahāvagga* (Vin I 305): a disciple admired the virtues of the naked ascetics and asked the Buddha permission to practice nakedness. He explained his intention in the following words: "Blessed One, you have praised in several ways those who are moderate in their desires, who are contented with little. You also praised those who have uprooted their defilements, who have tamed their passions, who are full of energy and devotion. Nakedness, Blessed One, is an efficient method, in various respects, to become moderate and contented with little, to uproot defilements, to tame the passions, to become pure, devoted and ardent. It would be good, Blessed One, to prescribe this practice for the whole Community." The Master immediately rejected his proposition. "This is not true, ignorant man," he said. "Nakedness would not be suitable for monks, but unworthy of them. This is not the right thing to do. How could you, ignorant man, adopt nakedness as it is practiced by other ascetics?" Clearly, nakedness was not acceptable to the Buddha because he deemed it unsuitable for monks; moreover, it was a practice common among other ascetics which people criticized. On other occasions, the Buddha forbade monks not only to practice nakedness as a virtue, but even to bathe naked in public (Vin II 121; for nuns, *Pācittiya* rule 21). Other ascetic modes of dress were also prohibited to Buddhist monks and nuns (Vin I 305).

Without a distinctive dress, they risked being confused with other ascetics. There are several stories in which Buddhist monks were mistaken for naked ascetics: once when some of them were bathing naked (see Vin I 291), and another time when they had their robes stolen by some highway robbers between Sāketa and Sāvatthi (Vin III 211–212). As we saw before, monks were not allowed to ask lay people for robes or pieces of cloth unless they were very close relatives or devoted followers. This is why, after their robes had beens stolen, the monks had to carry on their way naked, as they could not find the right people to ask for clothes. When he heard about this incident, the Master modified the rules in the following words:

> Monks, when robes are stolen or destroyed, in that case, I allow you to ask some from any man or woman, even if they are not close relatives or devoted followers. If this happens

> near a monastery, you must go there and take a robe from that monastery (*vihāra-cīvara*[5]), or a bed cover, or a piece of cloth used as a carpet or as a mattress-cover. I allow you to use them for a temporary period. . . If there is no monastery in the vicinity, or if you cannot find a robe there or . . . (as above), in that case you must cover yourself temporarily with grass or leaves. In no case must you go naked. If a monk goes naked, he is guilty of breaking the law"
>
> (Vin III 212).

One can see how vigorously confusion with other "renouncers," especially the naked ascetics, was avoided in Buddhist monasticism. Monks were not allowed to give the Ordination, whether minor or major, to candidates who came without begging-bowl and without a complete outfit of three robes (Vin I 90, cf. M III 247). If a naked ascetic asked to be allowed into the Community, a monk had first to be designated as his preceptor, and one of the preceptor's tasks was to find robes for the newcomer (Vin I 71). If an ascetic from another religious sect asked to be admitted to the Community, he had to undergo a probationary period of at least four months, in order to learn the behavior customary in the Community (Vin I 69). In this way, through their discipline in general, and in particular the adoption of suitable dress, Buddhist monks and nuns avoided being confused with other ascetics.

Another specific characteristic of Buddhist monks which the Buddha wished them to show by their manner of dress was correctness. According to the *Mahāvagga,* a monk revealed his sobriety in his behavior. On all occasions when he had to appear before lay people outside of the monastery or the residence, he had to dress fully, wearing his three robes. The rule was laid down as follows: "No monk is allowed to enter the village wearing only the *uttarāsaṅga* or the *antarāvāsaka.* If a monk goes there without wearing his three robes, he breaks the law" (Vin I 298). Monks could wear just one or two robes only in certain situations: when they were staying on their own in a residence, when they wanted to cross a river, when they fell ill or were resting in a room or cell whose door was locked, and also while they were looking for a new robe. They were not to leave their robes lying anywhere, and were not to leave the monastery with only two robes unless they were ill or had permission from the Community to do so (*Nissagiya Pācittiya* rule 2, Vin III 198–200, nuns' *Nissaggiya Pācittiya* 14). To prevent their robes being blown up by the wind, monks and nuns were obliged to knot together its two lower corners before leaving the monastery (Vin II 136–137). A strip of cloth called *kāyabandhana* served as a belt; its use was permitted by the Buddha after a rather comical incident. According to the *Cullavagga* (Vin II 135), a monk was walking one day along the road without a belt when his undergarment fell on the floor. At the sight people burst out laughing and the monk felt very embarrassed. When he heard about it, the Master required every monk to wear a belt made of cloth. Nuns were not allowed to leave their dwelling without a vest (*Pācittiya* rule 96 from the *Bhikkhunīvibhaṅga*, Vin IV 345). This rule was the consequence of an incident very similar to the previous one: one day a nun happened to go to a village to beg, without wearing her vest (or bodice). As she walked along the street, her top robe was blown up by the wind. People exclaimed, "beautiful is the breast of (this) nun!" and the nun, ridiculed in this way, felt very ashamed. So the Master forbade nuns to leave the monastery without wearing a vest.

Any carelessness in the matter of outward appearance, and especially of clothes, was severely reprimanded. The *Pātimokkha* contains 75 rules of good behavior (called *sekhiya dhammā*); the first ones emphasize the proprieties which must be observed by monks and nuns in their dress. They specify the following details:

> The undergarment must be properly wrapped around your waist. If you do not show proper care and put on your underrobe so that it hangs down at the front or back, you are guilty of breaking the law. You must wrap the top robe around your body so that both edges are in line. If you do not exercise

> proper care and put on your top robe so that it hangs down at the front or back, you are guilty of breaking the law. You must go to people's houses (to beg) properly dressed in your robes. If you do not exercise proper care and go to people's houses when you are not properly dressed, you are breaking the law . . . (and so on).

These rules of conduct were expressly prescribed not only to monks residing in monasteries or residences in villages or towns, but also to those who lived in the forest. When a robe was torn, it was not to be worn again before it was mended. For that purpose, monks and nuns were allowed to own a sewing kit: thread, sewing needle, a pattern for cutting cloth, etc.

Rules Concerning Acceptance and Possession of Robes

As the Community gained in popularity, and as the Buddha gave monks permission to accept robes or pieces of cloth from lay people, all kinds of fabrics accrued to the Community. The *Mahāvagga* (Vin I 280) tells of the enthusiasm with which lay followers responded to the Buddha's permission:

> When the people from the town of Rajagaha heard that the Buddha had allowed monks to accept robes given by householders (*gahapati-cīvara*), they were overcome with joy and excitement: "now we will give robes, and we will gain merit! . . ." In a single day, several thousand robes were given to the Community in the town of Rājagaha. People living in the surrounding countryside, when they heard of the permission given by the Buddha, also gave several hundred robes to the Community.

As in the case of lodgings and food, lay people believed that giving robes to monks and nuns would earn them merit. At the end of a sermon by the Buddha or his disciples, followers would express their satisfaction with gifts of robes or cloth (see M II 117). One day the wives of king Udena from Kosambi came to hear the venerable Ānanda preach the Doctrine, and at the end of his sermon, they gave him five hundred robes. When the king heard of this, he was annoyed by their prodigality, and politely asked Ānanda what was the use of such a great quantity of robes. Ānanda told him that the robes would be distributed among those monks who needed them and that they would make use of them with the utmost ingenuity, first as robes and then in many other ways, until they were worn down to shreds only good enough to mop the floor. The king was delighted with this answer and gave Ānanda another five hundred robes (Vin II 291). This story indirectly shows how monks were to get as much use as possible out of the robes given by lay people.

The generosity of lay people increased rapidly, and monks received large quantities of gifts every day. Rules had to be established in order to prevent abuse of this kindness, and to make clear how to benefit from it correctly and appropriately. The basic and general rule was that monks and nuns were not allowed to ask for robes or material from anyone, man or woman. In the *Bhikkhu-vibhaṅga* (Vin III 210–212), seven special amendments further specify this general rule. In no case, even if he had not received enough cloth to make a robe, was a monk allowed to make suggestions or demands. He was not allowed to make his preferences known in the matter of robes or fabrics, nor to seek the help of several benefactors in order to obtain a better robe (Vin III 216). *Nissaggiya Pācittiya* rule 10 forbade monks (*Nissaggiya Pācittiya* 20 for nuns) to accept money in place of a robe. If a lay follower offered money to a monk, the latter had to designate a servant who would accept the money for him and use it in a way which respected the donor's intention. The monk was not allowed to tell the servant what kind of robe he preferred. If the servant did not perform the transaction according to the wishes of the benefactor, if, for example he did not give the monk a robe, the monk was not allowed to quarrel with him (Vin III 218–222). Monks were not allowed to ask for cloth or yarn (*Nissaggiya Pācittiya* 26, Vin III 256, nuns' *Nissaggiya Pācittiya* 27). If a benefactor gave some yarn to a weaver for a robe, the monk for whom it was intended was not allowed to bribe or otherwise influence the weaver in order to obtain a robe to his taste.

All these different regulations were not simply designed to protect monks from the overbearing generosity of some lay people. They were also laid down in order to safeguard the essential spirit of renunciation through detachment from material things. Monks and nuns were not allowed to own more robes than was strictly necessary, and the use of an extra robe was an offense (*Nissaggiya Pācittiya* rule 1, Vin III 195, nuns' *Nissaggiya Pācittiya* 13).[6] If a monk accepted an extra robe, he was allowed to give it to another monk who needed a new one (that is, whose own robe was old or worn out). Once a monk had promised a robe to another monk in this way, he was not to make use of it any more (Vin IV 121), but had to hand it over within a maximum of ten days (Vin I 289, III 195). In the same way, it was not permitted to keep a piece of cloth given for a robe for more than thirty days (Vin III 203). Many rules emphasize the fact that monks should limit themselves to three robes.

Private Property and Communal Property

Monks' lodgings and furniture belonged to the Community, but clothes belonged to those who wore them. Monks were allowed to accept lay people's gifts of robes in their own name. Their three robes were regarded as their personal property. All new robes were to be marked so as to be recognizable by their owners (*Pācittiya* rule 59, Vin IV 120, nuns' *Pācittiya* 140). As for gifts of cloth, monks and nuns were not only allowed to accept them for themselves, they were also allowed to make a personal present of them to their father or mother if they were old or poor (Vin I 297). Although the robes worn by each monk were regarded as his personal property, monks were in the habit of exchanging robes. The Buddha himself gave his old robe to his disciple Mahā-Kassapa in exchange for Mahā-Kassapa's new one. The disciple gave it to him and accepted the Master's old robe with great respect (S II 121). The venerable Ānanda also wore for a few days a robe belonging to the venerable Sāriputta (Vin I 289). Nuns were also allowed to exchange robes among themselves (*Nissaggiya Pācittiya* rule 3 from the *Bhikkunī-vibhaṅga*), but they could not revoke the exchange once it was completed (Vin IV 246). The same rule applied to monks (*Nissaggiya Pācittiya* rule 25, Vin III 254). Nuns were forbidden to wear another nuns's robe without her permission (*Pācittiya* rule 25, Vin IV 281).

As people gave more and more robes to the Community, it became necessary to establish rules about communal ownership of them; the story of how these rules came to be laid down is told at length in the *Mahāvagga*. In many respects, this account is parallel to that of the development of regulations about food which occurred during times of famine in Rājagaha. As monks were limited to three robes, and would not accept any extra robes presented to them, lay people grew discontented and started to criticize their attitude. When he heard this, the Buddha decreed that a monk should be appointed to be in charge of receiving robes given by lay people. The monks who were first elected to be responsible for accepting gifts left them unattended in various places, where they became damaged, so that again people criticized them. The Master then decreed that a monk should be appointed to look after the robes. They kept them in the shade, at the feet of trees or in tree-hollows, as they were not allowed to keep them inside the monastery; but the robes were eaten by rats and white ants, and once more people criticized the monks. So the Master allowed them to set aside a room inside the monastery to store the robes. But the robes which were deposited there with the approval of the Community in time became spoiled. So the Buddha allowed monks to appoint a monk to be in charge of the store. Robes given to the Community piled up in the store, but there was nobody to distribute them. Finally the Buddha allowed monks to appoint a monk responsible for distributing the robes, and for sharing them out among those members of the Community who needed them. A monk had to possess five qualities to be elected to these offices by the Community: he had to be one who would not distribute robes incorrectly, through partiality, hatred, fear or stupidity, and who knew what should and should not be done (Vin I 283–285).

Extra robes were regarded as common property. No monk was allowed to use them, distribute them or give them away on his own authority. Lay followers became more and more accustomed to give robes or cloth to the Community rather than to individual monks. The Buddha encouraged this trend. One day, his step-mother, Mahāpajāpatī Gotamī, brought him a piece of costly material as a gift; but instead of accepting it for himself, the Buddha insisted that she should give it to the Community, explaining to her that a gift to the Community is always better that a gift to an individual person (M III 253–254). Monks were not allowed to take for themselves anything given to the Community (*Nissaggiya Pācittiya* rule 30, nuns' *Nissaggiya Pācittiya* 30). This rule was established after a monk tried to claim for himself some fabrics given to the Community (Vin III 265).

Dress Accessories

BATHING ROBES

It was improper for monks and nuns to bathe naked. At the request of Visākhā, a great benefactress of the Community, the Buddha ruled that nuns should wear a bathing-robe (*udakasāṭikā*) when bathing. Furthermore, the *Mahāvagga* tells us that Visākhā was always ready to provide nuns with cloth for bathing-robes (Vin I 293). In her opinion, "nakedness in a woman was shameful and blameworthy," so she made the following proposition to the Buddha: "Blessed One, I wish for the rest of my life to provide nuns with bathing-robes." The rule forbidding nuns to bathe naked (*Pācittiya* 21, Vin IV 278, cf. Vin I 293) was established as a result of an incident at the River Aciravatī, where the sight of young nuns bathing had displeased some people.

Visākhā also criticized nakedness in men (Vin I 297). She wished to provide monks with rain garments (*vasakasāṭika*), which seem also to have been used for bathing. They were to be made one month before the beginning of the rainy season (*Nissaggiya Pācittiya* rule 24, Vin III 252); this has led some scholars to think that they were used only during the rainy season, as an extra robe against the rain. However, the circumstances in which "rain garments" were first used suggest that they were in fact intended for bathing: the Buddha recommended them after some monks had bathed naked in the yard of the Jetavana monastery during the rainy season. When she heard about it, Visākhā offered to provide monks with "rain garments," and the Buddha accepted (Vin I 292).[7] The rule established a limited period during which rain garments were to be made, one month before the rainy season; the intention seems to have been to prevent monks from seeking new fabrics all year round.

Monks and nuns suffering from skin diseases were permitted to use another small piece of cloth, called *kaṇḍupaṭichādi* in the *Vinaya*, measuring 3′ by 2′3″ (*Pācittiya* rule 90, Vin IV 295, nuns' *Pācittiya* 165). Once when the Master was making a tour of monasteries and residences with the venerable Ānanda, he saw that the beds were rather dirty. He allowed monks the use of a piece of cloth to protect their bodies, as well as their robes and beds; at first it was to measure 1′6″ by 1′2″ (*Pācittiya* 89, Vin IV 171), but soon afterwards, the Master modified the rule and permitted the use of sheets of adequate dimensions (Vin I 295).

GARMENTS AND MATERIAL MADE OF WOOL

Soon after the Buddha had allowed monks to accept robes and fabrics, the Community was given a woollen coat, along with a silk coat and a fleecy coverlet. The Buddha permitted monks to accept them (Vin I 281). One day it happened that Jīvaka Komārabacca, the royal doctor, brought the Buddha a piece of woollen material sent by the king of the Kāsi country. The Buddha accepted it and at the same time allowed monks to accept woollen material, to be used for winter robes. Monks and nuns could also use blankets, but to insure moderation their value had to be limited. Nuns looking for a winter blanket had to find one worth less that 16 *kahāpaṇa,* and one worth less than 10 *kahāpaṇa* for the other seasons. (A *kahāpaṇa* was a unit of money: see Chapter 5; pp. 85–6). A nun using a more costly blanket committed an offense (*Nissaggiya Pācittiya* rules 11 and 12, Vin IV 255–257). We do not know whether these blankets were the personal property of monks and nuns, nor is there any way to ascertain whether they took them away with them when traveling. It seems more likely that blankets and other such articles were common property of the Community, to be left in monasteries and residences.

SHOES

A whole chapter of the *Mahāvagga* is devoted to shoes. At first, monks and nuns did not wear shoes: permission to wear them was first given to a monk called Soṇa-Kolīvisa because of a personal problem he had. He was a very wealthy young man who had joined the Community and showed great courage in his religious practice. But he had very delicate feet which he hurt continually in walking meditation, and the wounds bled on the meditation walkway. When he saw this, the Master allowed him to wear sandals made of a single strand; but being the only one in the Community to enjoy such a privilege, Soṇa-Kolīvisa was reluctant to wear his sandals. In order to put him at ease, the Master extended the rule to the whole Community (Vin I 182–184). This permission was modified several times later on.

As a rule, monks were not allowed to wear sandals inside the monastery, including the yard and the garden. The *Mahāvagga* gives the reason for this: wearing sandals could be a sign of disrespect towards older monks; and the noise of sandals could disrupt their meditation. On the other hand if someone had sore feet or was ill, he could always wear sandals, even inside the monastery (Vin I 187, III 337). To avoid dirtying their beds, monks were allowed to wear sandals on their way to bed, after they had washed their feet. If they had to walk through the monastery yard in darkness, they could put sandals on to avoid hurting their feet against tree roots. Wooden sandals or clogs, on the contrary, were strictly forbidden: their clatter would disrupt the monks' contemplation, and the wood risked hurting small living creatures. As for sandals made of bamboo or palm-tree leaves, they were prohibited because they involved the destruction of plant life. Monks were not to go begging with their sandals on, unless they were ill (Vin I 194). Those who lived in forests or woods had to take off their sandals when they entered a village to beg. They owned a bag to carry them in (Vin II 217). A sick monk or nun, however, was allowed to keep his sandals on in the village (Vin I 194, III 337).

These permissions and prohibitions concerning shoes were the result of purely pragmatic and social considerations. Another kind of consideration led to the prohibition of certain types of sandals. As is related in the *Mahāvagga,* a group of monks from the town of Bhaddiya were wearing sandals made of grass or wood, as well as shoes decorated with gold, precious stones, crystal and so on. The Buddha asked his disciples: "How is it that these monks from Bhaddiya wear such sandals and decorated shoes . . . and neglect the discipline, the higher virtue, the higher concentration and the higher wisdom?" (Vin I 190) On this occasion, the Master told his disciples that to wear such shoes was not to follow the "middle way," and did not help inner progress. The Buddha forbade monks to wear decorated shoes, as well as multicolored sandals, even when made of a single strand (Vin I 185).

The Master did not hesitate to modify the rules to make the life of monks and nuns easier in different climatic and social conditions. For example, the original rule only allowed sandals made of a single strand. The venerable Mahā-Kaccāna lived in Avanti; he sent his pupil Soṇa-Kuṭikanna to the Buddha in Sāvatthi with the following request: "Blessed One, the earth in Avanti is black and hard, it is trampled down by cattle's feet. The roads are very rough, and sandals made of a single strand are not sufficient. It would be a good idea, Blessed One, to allow sandals made with more than one strand." (See Chapter 2, p. 29.) The Master called the monks together and modified several rules, not only for Avanti, but for other countries as well (Vin I 195). Thereafter monks were allowd to wear sandals made with several strands.

PARASOLS AND WALKING STICKS

At first monks were allowed to use a parasol; but the permission was later restricted to the monastery yard as a result of criticisms by lay people. The use of a parasol was generally a sign of wealth and power in the society of that time. One day, a group of monks was walking along the road carrying parasols, when a naked ascetic ironically remarked to a lay Buddhist; "look, my friend, your venerables are coming along with their parasols, like some great dignitaries!" The incident led to the prohibition of parasols outside the monastery yard (Vin II 130). Monks and nuns who were ill, however, were allowed to carry parasols even outside the monastery yards (Vin II 131, IV 337).

Walking sticks were only allowed in some cases. Monks who were weak or ill could use one if they received permission from the Community to do so. They had to present their request in a manner formally laid down in the *Vinaya*. Before a formal gathering of the Community, they had to express themselves respectfully in the following words: "Venerable ones, I am ill, I am not able to walk without a walking stick. I wish, venerable ones, to be accepted by the Community as one who needs a walking stick, and I ask your permission to use one" (Vin II 131). The reason for this restriction is easy to understand: carrying a stick in the streets was a sign of power. A stick was also an instrument of violence and therefore unsuitable for monks who had embraced non-violence. The *Nikāya* texts (D I 63; A II 208) describe a disciple of the Buddha as one who has abandoned sticks and weapons. Before the rule was laid down a monk with a walking stick had once been mistaken for a thief in a village (Vin II 131). The unrestricted use of a walking stick was therefore not allowed.

ENDNOTES

1. This celebrated doctor, the personal physician of King Bimbisāra, ministered to the king himself, and also to the Buddha and his Community.
2. *Siveyyaka* denotes a kind of material woven by the skilled women of a country called Sivi.
3. In the practice of modern Theravāda Buddhist monks, their sizes are:

	Length	Width	Size
Saṅghāṭi	108 in.	72 in.	6¼ sq. yds.
Uttarāsaṅga	108 in.	72 in.	6¼ sq. yds.
Antarāvāsaka	78 in.	42 in.	2½ sq. yds.

4. Devadatta was the Buddha's cousin, and became one of his religious disciples. Later he became more and more extremist, and finally left the Buddha.
5. According to the *Vinaya* commentary (p.666), *vihāra-cīvara* refers to robes left in dwellings or monasteries by lay people for monks who might have need of them.
6. In certain conditions they could wear an extra robe, for a period of ten days at the most.
7. The "rain garment" is a rectangular piece of cloth measuring 4′6″ by 2′3″.

Chapter 4

Food

As a bee gathers nectar from a flower and flies away without harming its color or scent, so is a wise man to live in a village (Dhp 49).

According to the canonical texts, Buddhist monks and nuns embraced the religious life "after putting aside the sickle and the flail" (M II 180; A III 5). This symbolic phrase means that they gave up working for a living. From the monastic point of view, it is not essential to earn one's living; on the contrary, professional work is a source of attachment to material things and of involvement with the world. Some scholars hold the view that ascetics living at the time of the Buddha did not engage in manual labor, and that the Buddha, therefore, simply conformed to the customs of other religious traditions in forbidding his monastic disciples to work. But although there were many renouncers at the time who did not do manual work, one should not over-generalize. Canonical texts also speak of wealthy ascetics earning a good living. The *Jātaka* stories mention ascetics living in forests far away from human habitation, and surviving on roots and fruit; sometimes they did a little farming. Some stories show them tending cows for milk and butter. In fact, Buddhist monasticism did not forbid manual labor such as sweeping or repairing the monastery, for example, but any kind of work intended to earn a living, whether manual or not; any kind of lucrative work is regarded as incompatible with the religious life.

According to the canonical texts, there were ascetics and

brahmins at the time of the Buddha who earned their living in various ways apart from manual labor. In the *Sāmaññaphala-sutta* (D I 67–69, cf. D I 9–12) they are shown making a living from the interpretation of bodily signs, stars, dreams, and rat-inflicted wounds, from the performance of sacrifices and offerings of all kinds, and from the practice of various "sciences", of demons, snakes, auspicious building-sites, and so on. The Buddha regarded these things as "vulgar (literally, bestial) knowledge" (*tiracchāna vijjā*) and "wrong livelihood" (*micchā ājīva*). He asserted on several occasions that they could only corrupt the clarity and purity of the religious life (Vin II 295; M III 75; A II 53). Earning goods and money, making a profit, and exploiting the miraculous powers given by inner progress in order to gain profit and material goods, were all activities condemned in Buddhist monasticism. One day, for example, the venerable Piṇḍola Bhāradvāja Thera displayed his miraculous powers to a crowd in Rājagaha, in order to win a sandalwood bowl placed at the top of a bamboo cane by a wealthy merchant of the town. Several non-Buddhist ascetics had failed to get hold of the bowl, but Piṇḍola Bhāradvāja succeeded. The spectators were very pleased, but the Buddha sternly criticized the behavior of his disciple:

> That was not the right thing to do. That was not the proper thing to do for a monk. How could you, Bhāradvāja, display your extraordinary miraculous powers in public, all for the sake of a worthless wooden bowl? Just as whore exhibits herself for the sake of money, so you displayed your miraculous powers in public for the sake of a worthless wooden bowl.

As a result, the Master forbade monks to display their miraculous powers (Vin II 112). His reasons are easy to understand: he did not want to encourage his disciples to gain material profit from the extraordinary powers conferred upon them by inner progress. He also wanted to prevent them from entering the path of inner progress in order to acquire miraculous powers and to use them for material profit, like magicians. The *Mahāsāropama-sutta* (M I 192ff.) states explicitly that the life of purity taught by the Buddha does not aim at profit, honor or fame.

Other means of earning a living which lay people felt were suitable for ascetics were also forbidden to Buddhist monks. A monk intent on extreme ascetic practices had settled in a burial-ground; there he lived a contemplative life, feeding on food left under trees for their ancestors by visitors to the ground. He thought that his way of life showed great virtue, but the Buddha thought it improper, and forbade monks to eat food in burial-grounds (Vin IV 90).

If Buddhist monks and nuns were not to work for a living or follow a trade, how could they feed themselves? *Pācittiya* rule 40 (Vin IV 90; cf. nuns' *Pācittiya* 122) gives us the answer:

> Monks must not eat food which they have not received from someone else's hands. If a monk does eat food which he has not received from someone else's hands, he commits an offense in the *Pācittiya* category.

So monks and nuns were only allowed to eat what they had been given. They were not to provide themselves with food. Even if they chanced upon some food, they were not allowed to eat it. In this matter they were completely dependent on others, like small children or hospitalized sick people. They had two ways of obtaining food: they could beg from house to house, or be invited to eat by lay followers.

Begging for Alms

We do not know whether all ascetics at the time of the Buddha were mendicants, begging for alms from door to door, but we do know that some of them were. According to the canonical texts, when the ascetic Gotama came to Rājagaha from his native country, before his Enlightenment and even before his period of extreme austerities, he started begging in the streets of the town. The *Sutta Nipata* (Sn 408) describes how astonished the citizens of Rājagaha were at the sight of the new young renouncer. After his Enlightenment, Gotama the Buddha went to Kapilavatthu, and begged for alms with his disciples in front of the house of the proud Sākyans, his relatives.

Although begging was not a new practice in society at that time, it was not regarded by all lay people as a respectable way of life. For example, when the Buddha was begging in the streets of Kapilavatthu, his father expressed disapproval: 'begging for alms is bad for the Sākyans' reputation.' Once the Buddha begged at the door of a wealthy brahmin called Kasī Bhāradvāja, who was performing a thanksgiving sacrifice for the harvest; instead of giving him something, the brahmin flew into a temper: "You shaven head! You would do better to work rather than beg. Look at me! I plow and sow; when I have plowed and sowed, I can eat. If you did the same, you would have something to eat" (Sn pp. 12ff.). The *Piṇḍa-sutta* tells us that once the Buddha was not given any food in a brahmin village (S i 167). The venerable Raṭṭhapāla Thera was begging in his native town; his father, a wealthy householder, saw him and was saddened by the "wretched" circumstances of his only son's life (M II 61). When the Arahant Sāriputta Thera visited his mother with his pupil, the novice Rāhula, the old brahmin woman started to wail and berate her son as a garbage-eater (Dhp–a IV 164). Another brahmin angrily asked his daughter: "why do you give food to those shaven-headed priestlings who won't do any work to earn their living?" (Thī 273). Thus many people were hostile to begging, notably orthodox brahmins who thought it degrading. Some brahmins who joined the Community in their old age did not want to beg (Vin I 57), but they had to conform to the customs of the Community. The Buddha believed that begging was the "right livelihood" (*sammā ājīva*) for renouncers.

Monks went in search of alms with a begging bowl (Vin II 215–217). They would stand in silence in front of the donor's door: if they were given something, they were to accept it regardless of quality or quantity. If they were not given anything, they were not to feel displeasure, sadness or frustration. When they were given something, they were not to look at the donor's face, nor to try and find out whether it was a man or a woman. They were to wear their robes correctly when begging, and the robes had to be clean. As they walked on their begging-round, they were to control their senses and practice mindfulness (Vin II 215–216, M III 293), and they were asked not to sit down in the donor's house while on a begging tour (Vin IV 94). This last rule was intended to prevent improper friendships arising between monks and their male or female benefactors.

In lay people's eyes, Buddhist monks were not beggars or tramps: this was obvious from their dress and behavior. They were "renouncers," on the path of inner progress. Most of them came from rich families, having renounced their luxurious life. So lay people gave them food with respect, and addressed them in the most respectful terms. For their part, monks and nuns were not to prompt their benefactors in any way; when begging, they were not to utter any request, nor express any preferences. Lay followers regarded it as their duty, as lay disciples of the Buddha, to provide for them; and besides, they earned merit in doing so, for the monks and nuns represented a Community which was "worthy of offerings, worthy of hospitality, worthy of gifts, worthy of respect; the greatest field of merit in the world" (M III 81; A IV 406).

Being Invited to Eat in Lay Households

Canonical and post-canonical texts call a Buddhist monk a *bhikkhu* and a nun a *bhikkhunī*, that is to say a "beggar of alms," or a "religious mendicant."[1] But this does not mean that they always begged for their food; they would also be invited to eat by lay followers. In that case, one might ask, why were they called *bhikkhu* and *bhikkhunī*? The term refers to their detachment from worldly things, rather than to actual begging, which is only a consequence of renunciation.[2]

According to the canonical texts, begging was not mandatory; there are no rules in the *Pātimokkha* which specifically require it. Nonetheless, all candidates for the major Ordination were symbolically reminded of the custom of begging, in order to emphasize the simplicity of the monastic life (Vin I 58).

Devadatta, in his enthusiasm for extreme practices, asked the Master to establish the following rule: "every monk must subsist simply on the alms he has received in his begging-bowl and no monk is allowed to accept an invitation to eat in someone's house" (Vin II 197). The Master refused Devadatta's proposal. He did not want to establish a rule restricting his disciples to begging for their subsistence. So they were invited to eat in lay households. When the Buddha arrived in Rājagaha soon after his Enlightenment, he was invited to eat with his disciples by king Bimbisāra, and he accepted (Vin I 38). There are many such examples in the canonical texts. Discussions between the Buddha and lay people often ended with an invitation to eat; both those who were already supporters of the Buddha and those whom he had defeated in debate would ask him: "Blessed One, may you accept to come and eat in my house with your disciples tomorrow." The Buddha accepted by remaining silent; but if he had already been invited by someone else, he declined the second invitation (Vin I 232). The next day, towards midday when the meal was ready, the host would come in person or send a messenger: "Blessed One, it is time, the meal is ready." Then the Buddha would put on his robes, take his begging bowl and proceed to his host's house with his disciples (D I 109–110, 148; II 88, 95, 97, 126–127, etc.).

Some lay disciples always kept their houses ready to receive monks and nuns, however many there were. Every day, for example, Visākhā-Migāra-Mātā, a great benefactress of the new Community, would feed a hundred or so monks who came to her house without invitation before noon (Dhp-a I 28). She undertook to provide food all her life for monks who had just arrived at the town of Sāvatthi, or were passing through (Vin I 292).

It seems that the desire to earn merit was at the root of lay charity. People had started to invite monks and nuns to eat in their houses long before they would come begging to their doors. They saw it as a better way of earning merit than giving alms in front of the house. Inviting monks to eat was also a way of showing respect towards the Community (M II 380). The Buddha did not fail to spell out the results of such acts of generosity. One day he told a high dignitary from Benares, who had invited him to eat:

> Friend, on the day when you invited the Community headed by the Buddha, on that day you earned much merit. And on the day when monks received a ball of rice from your hand, on that day you earned much merit. Heaven will be your reward (Vin I 223).

How could Buddhist monks and nuns possibly remain faithful to their ideal of renunciation, if they were accustomed to eat in lay households? Why did they accept these invitations instead of begging? From the point of view of Buddhist monasticism, both practices were equally good, since the primary rule was to eat only food received from others. As we saw earlier, monks were not permitted to eat food unless someone gave it to them (*Pācittiya* rule 40, nuns' *Pācittiya* 122). They were to accept and eat whatever was put in their bowl, whether they were begging from door to door or had been invited to eat. Thus both customs were equally legitimate and consistent with the rules.

As far as invitations to eat were concerned, all the details were foreseen and codified in the *Vinaya*. A personal invitation was not acceptable. Lay followers could not invite one monk, a few monks or a group of monks; they could only address their invitation to the Community, which then chose which monks to send on such and such a day to such and such a house (Vin IV 71). This rule (*Pācittiya* rule 32, nuns' *Pācittiya* 118), however, was modified several times as customs evolved. According to its last revision, there were special times when monks were allowed to accept invitations to eat in groups of two or three: in times of sickness, when robes were distributed, when robes were prepared, when traveling or embarking on a boat, and in times of famine. Other rules from the *Pātimokkha* established priorities among different invitations. After accepting an invitation, a monk who was not able to go had to send someone else in his stead. If he did not go himself and did not send someone else, and had nevertheless accepted another invitation, he committed an offense (*Pācittiya* rule 33, Vin IV 76).

For eating, monks and nuns always used their begging-bowls, whether they had begged the food or had been invited to eat. The begging-bowl was a symbol of their special mendicancy. They, like the Buddha, used them both to receive food and to eat from. They were only allowed to receive alms in their bowl. This prohibition was intended to differentiate Buddhist monks and nuns from the members of other sects, some of whom had very unusual customs. The *Cullavagga* (Vin II 112–114) describes some of them accepting food directly in their hands, others on the ground, others in a water jug; some even used a skull. The Buddha forbade these practices, and decreed that his disciples should take food in their bowl. The begging-bowl was to be made of iron or clay; gold, silver, bronze, glass, and wood were not allowed. When his begging-bowl became worn out, a monk could get another one from the Community, but the old one had to be clearly worn through in five different places (*Nissaggiya Pācittiya* 21 and 22, Vin III 242–247, nuns' *Nissaggiya Pācittiya* 24). Monks were forbidden to introduce into the Community someone who did not have a begging-bowl of his own (Vin I 90, cf. M III 247).

The Development of Rules Concerning Food

In time, as the Community increased in number, it became necessary to amend the first rules laid down in the *Vinaya* according to various climatic and social conditions. As a legislator, the Buddha seems to have been prepared to consider any request made by members of his new Community, and did not hesitate to revise and amend existing rules. There were two reasons for this: he was always concerned with the well-being of his disciples, and he did not want to lead them on a path of extreme self-mortification. Buddhist monastic discipline included both prohibitions and well-defined limits to prohibition; this is most notable in that section of the *Vinaya piṭaka* called *Khandhaka* (the *Mahāvagga* and the *Cullavagga*). In these texts, rules about food were modified in three main areas: monks were appointed to take charge of food, permission was given to store and cook food, and special dispensations were given to those going on a journey.

(i) *Monks in charge of food*. According to the *Cullavagga*, some monks were appointed by the Community to deal with certain problems arising in connection with food. One of the most important of these was the "dispenser of meals." As we saw above, if a lay follower wished to invite monks to eat, he had to address his invitation to the Community; then a certain number of its members would be chosen, the ones deemed most suitable to go and eat at that particular house. No one was to choose the house at which he would eat. At the special times when lay followers were allowed to invite monks in groups of two or three (see pp. 62–3), they were still not allowed to choose which monks to invite. Naturally, these rules gave rise to conflicts between monks and even between lay followers. To avoid them, it was necessary to defer matters to a monk who would be impartial and prudent in coming to a judgment. Such a monk, the "dispenser of meals," was appointed to choose which monks to send to which house (Vin II 175).

According to the Cullavagga, other monks were in charge of distributing rice gruel, solid food, and fruit. Lastly there was the "store-keeper." The responsibilities of these "superintendent-monks" pose another question: if monks were to live simply on alms received while begging or when being invited, why did they need these officers? The answer is that another way of obtaining food developed in time: it could also be brought to the monastery by lay followers (Vin I 220–21). The custom probably started in a time of hardship. When monks in charge of food are first mentioned in the *Cullavagga,* "at that time there was not enough food in Rājagaha, because of a drought" (Vin II 175).

(ii) *Permission to store and to cook food.* At first monks did not store food or cook meals. After a meal, no food was kept for the next day. In fact, storing food was prohibited (*Pācittiya* 38). This rule was laid down as the result of a monk's misdemeanour; he was called Ballaṭṭhisīsa, and often lived in a forest hut. As he did not want to go begging every day, he only went some days and then dried the rice to eat it on the other days. So *Pācittiya* rule 38 was established: a monk who eats or shares food that he has kept commits a *Pācittiya* offense (Vin IV 86; nuns' *Pācittiya* 121). On the other hand, a sick monk was allowed to keep five kinds food, for a maximum of a week: ghee (clarified melted butter), fresh butter, sesame oil, honey and molasses (*Nissaggiya Pācittiya* rule 23, Vin III 251, nuns' *Nissaggiya Pācittiya* 25).

Cooking food was also prohibited. One day the venerable Ānanda prepared some gruel for the Master, but was rebuked for it. The Master did not regard cooking as fit for monks: "Food cooked in the monastery must not be consumed. Monks who cook in the monastery, or who eat what has been cooked there are guilty of breaking the law" (Vin I 211). However, when a famine occurred in Rājagaha, all these rules had to be amended. The story is recounted in the *Mahāvagga:* in that time of starvation, lay people brought salt, oil, husked rice and solid food to the monastery. Monks dried them outside the boundary of the monastery, but cats, mice and lizards ate them, and even thieves took some away. The monks told the Buddha, who answered them: "I allow you to dry food inside the monastery." Then the monks started to dry food inside the monastery, but they still had to cook outside its boundary, so that the people who lived in the vicinity would gather around the food. The monks reported this to the Buddha, who said: "monks, I allow you to cook inside the monastery." Now, cooking food for the monks was in those days the task of lay helpers, although monks may perhaps already have been allowed to warm up their food themselves. During times of famine, some lay helpers took some of the food given to the monks. So the Buddha cancelled another prohibition: "I allow you to do your cooking yourself; I also allow you to eat what has been dried and cooked in the monastery, and what you have cooked yourself" (Vin I 212). Thereafter, monks were able to cook food brought to the monastery by lay people during the famine. The appearance of monks responsible for distributing food, the permission to store food and to cook inside the monastery were three ways in which the Buddha adapted the Monastic Rule to the shortage of food. "Store-keepers" were required to look after what lay followers had brought, sometimes from very far away.

Monks sometimes received more food than they needed. In Vesāli, for example, lay followers gave them too much food, and the monks got into the habit of sharing it with the ascetics of other religious systems. One day, a naked ascetic, a Jain monk who had received food from Buddhist monks, made an ironical comment about them. Lay followers heard him and reported it to the Buddha. At their request, he forbade monks to give food with their own hands to ascetics from other religious groups (Vin IV 91). (According to *Pācittiya* rule 41 (nuns' *Pācittiya* 46), there is no offense if a monk or nun gets someone else to give the food, or if he or she leaves it for an ascetic to pick up.)

(iii) *Special dispensations for those going on a journey.* According to the texts of the Vinaya, at first Buddhist monks and nuns did not usually provide themselves with foodstuffs. Whether they stayed in a monastery or traveled between towns and villages, food was provided by lay followers. However, if they were to travel across large forests or deserts, they had to take some with them. According to the *Mahāvagga,* the Buddha was made aware of this necessity not by monks but by the great banker Meṇḍaka. Meṇḍaka told him: "Blessed one, there are roads in the desert where one finds little water and little food. It is not easy for monks to travel there without provisions. Blessed One, it would be good if you were to allow monks to take food items with them when traveling." Meṇḍaka was right. He made his request at a time when the Buddha and a large group of disciples were going from the town of Bhaddiya to Anguttarāpa. The banker had loaded food items in several carts and taken several helpers to prepare the food for "the group of monks headed by the Buddha," while they crossed the large forest laying between the two towns (Vin I 244). At Meṇḍaka's request, the Buddha allowed the following:

> There are roads in the desert where one finds little water and little food; it is difficult to travel there without provisions. Monks, I allow you to take food items with you for traveling. If you need husked rice, take husked rice; if you need dwarf beans, take dwarf beans; if you need salt, take salt;[3] if you need sugar, take sugar; if you need oil, take oil; if you need ghee, take ghee.

This permission does not mean that monks and nuns were always looking for food items; in fact the text specifies that habitually looking for and storing food was improper.

On the whole, monks had no problems finding food: they received a great deal. They were even given delicious meals. For example, a great banker of Rājagaha was organizing a meal for the Buddha and his disciples, whom he had invited for the next day. A great banker from Sāvatthi happened to visit him on that very day. Not knowing the reason for these preparations, he asked him "My friend, are you preparing the marriage ceremony of a son or daughter, or a great sacrifice? Are you about to receive the king of Magadha and his ministers for a meal tomorrow?" (Vin II 155). Similarly, when Keniya Jāṭila was preparing a meal for the Buddha and his disciples, the brahmin Sela asked "Are you preparing the marriage ceremony of a son or daughter?" (Sn pp. 104–5, cf. M II 146f.) As a result, other ascetics came to think that the Buddha's disciples were straying from the ideal of renunciation: an ascetic from the Jain Community called Buddhist monks "shaven-headed householders" (*muṇḍa gahapati*) (Vin IV 92). In the eyes of such critics, Buddhist monks lived in luxury. It is true that they did not follow a very strict regime. For all that, were they indulging in gluttony? Were there no restrictions on food in the rules?

Restrictions on the Consumption of Food: (1) Rules

Buddhist monks and nuns were only allowed to eat once a day: "If a monk (or nun) eats soft or solid food[4] outside the right time, he commits an offense from the *Pācittiya* category"; the "right time" was from sunrise to noon (*Pācittiya* 37, Vin IV 85, nuns' *Pācittiya* 120). The rule limiting meals to one a day applied both to fully ordained monks and nuns and to novices (Vin I 83). This may seem a rather harsh practice: it is hard to go without eating from noon until the next morning. But it is in keeping with the general spirit of asceticism. Nonetheless, this does not mean that all ascetics at the time would have specifically abstained from eating after noon. Even within the Buddhist Community some monks used to take food in the afternoon (Vin IV 85) before the rule about the "right time" to eat was established. A monk called Bhaddāli openly declared that he could not live without a meal in the evening (M I 437–8). Some monks living in Kīṭāgiri also ate in the evening. After the Buddha had detailed for them the disadvantages of eating after noon, and had established the rule about the "right time" to eat, they were obliged to limit themselves to one meal a day (M I 473ff; cf. M I 124, 448). The Buddha told them:

> Monks, I do not eat in the evening. Because I avoid eating in the evening, I am in good health, light, energetic and live comfortably. You too, monks, avoid eating in the evening, and you will have good health.

Moreover, if monks had had more than one meal a day, they would have wasted time begging or eating in people's houses, during the day and in the evening. It would necessarily have become an obstacle to their religious progress. Besides, if monks had stood in front of houses in the dark, in order to receive alms, people might have been frightened. The *Vinaya* tells us how one day a woman, seeing a monk standing outside her house in the dark, was scared and started to scream, thinking that he was a ghost (Vin II 115; cf. M I 447).

Pācittiya rule 39 laid down another important restriction: monks were forbidden to request or even to make known their favorite foods, and to eat any food that they might have received as a result of expressing such preferences:

> If a monk, who is not unwell, requests and eats delicacies such as curd, fresh butter, sesame oil, honey and molasses, fish, meat, milk, etc., he commits a *Pācittiya* offense (Vin IV 88).

Eight rules, entitled "offenses involving declaration and confession" (*Pāṭidesanīya āpatti*), forbade nuns to ask for specific foods; they too were not allowed to express their preferences for any food, to ask for it or to eat it (Vin IV 346–348). Four rules of the same category, concerning meals improperly obtained, applied to monks. These rules were designed to prevent gluttony in monks and nuns, compelling them to be content with what they had received, and to eat with sobriety. They were also intended to spare the Community's benefactors any difficulties. The aim was both to prevent monks and nuns from abusing their benefactors' generosity, and to encourage them to practice moderation.

What were the rules concerning eating fish or meat? "Monks must not eat meat, if the animal has been killed directly for them. If they do, they are guilty of breaking the Rule" (Vin I 238). It is obvious from this rule that there was no total ban on meat eating. Some other rules from the *Mahāvagga* (Vin I 219) prohibit eating the flesh of certain specific animals: elephant, horse, lion, snake and dog. Clearly, the fact that there were rules prohibiting specific kinds of meat shows that other kinds were permitted. From an ethical point of view, however, did not the permission to eat meat contradict the Buddhist principle of universal love? The Buddha exhorted monks to show love even to a dangerous enemy: "Even were someone to be carved up limb by limb with a double-handled saw, if he felt hate towards his attackers he would not be following my teaching" (*Kakacūpama-sutta*, M I 129). The *Sutta-nipāta* says: "as a mother will risk her life to protect her only child, so one should develop in one's mind a boundless love for all living beings, for the whole world, above, beneath and on all sides, with infinite loving-kindness" (Sn 143–152). Here Buddhism preaches respect not only for human beings, but for all living creatures. With this principle in mind, how can one eat meat? Why did the *Vinaya* rules not make vegetarianism compulsory?

It is true that Buddhist monasticism laid stress on universal love. Monks were not allowed to kill animals (*Pācittiya* rule 61, Vin IV 124, nuns' *Pācittiya* 142), or to use water in which small creatures were living (*Pācittiya* rule 62, nuns' *Pācittiya* 143). They had to expel any novice who killed animals (Vin I 85). In several sermons, the Buddha spoke against fishermen and fishmongers (A III 300; S IV 308; UD 51–56), and against butchers (A V 288; M I 39, 387, II 203; S II 254–256). Furthermore, he sternly criticized the contemporary brahmanical custom of animal sacrifice (D II 352–353, III 147; S I 76; A I 151, II 42, IV 41–46; Sn 79–86, 303; Dhp 261). Cultivating universal love is described in many texts as one of the four "sublime states of mind" (*brahma-vihāra;* e.g. D II 196, III 220). One who mistreats animals is not an *Ariya,* a "noble" (Dhp 270), whereas one who has compassion for all living beings deserves to be called an *Ariya*. Why then was there no total ban on eating meat for Buddhist renouncers?

The reason was the principle that monks and nuns had to obtain their food through begging or being invited to eat in lay households. They were not to ask anything of their donors, or to express their preferences. Thus they had to accept what was given to them, and could not influence what kinds of food they received. Moreover, monks and nuns were often strangers in the town or village where they begged for food, so that their donors did not know what they preferred; they gave them part of what they had already prepared for themselves. Therefore monks and nuns who received meat were not responsible for the fact that an animal had been killed. Of the Five Precepts intended for lay Buddhists, the first one was to "abstain from destroying life." Of course, lay followers who observed the precepts did not kill animals to feed them to members of the Community. So monks and nuns could safely assume that any meat they might happen to receive did not come from an animal killed on purpose for them; they could be certain that they were not connected with the killing of the animal. In this case, there was no logical difference between meat and vegetables.

The monk Devadatta proposed that a rule of strict vegetarianism should be established for the Community, but this was not accepted by the Master (Vin II 197). Such an extreme rule would have caused difficulties for monks and nuns begging in distant places. The Master explained his opposition to Devadatta's suggestion: if the monk who received meat and the donor who gave it to him were not responsible for killing the animal, if they had neither seen, heard, nor suspected that the animal had been killed on purpose for him, then the meat was pure; eating it was not an offense (Vin I 238; cf. M I 368–371). (Here "pure" means right, properly and lawfully obtained. In connection with food Buddhism uses the term "purity" in this sense, and not to denote the intrinsic nature of the food, as in Brahmanism.) Buddhism takes an objective approach: if there is no direct or indirect connection between the killing of the animal and the monk eating its meat, then he is not committing an offense. This is why there was no total prohibition on eating meat in Buddhist monasticism.

Other rules prohibited monks to go and eat in certain places. For example, they were not allowed to go and eat in a place where people had organized a food distribution for the old, the sick, the poor and also for non-Buddhist ascetics. Monks could only obtain food at such a place if they were ill, and then only once (*Pācittiya* rule 31, Vin IV 69–70, nuns'

Pācittiya 117). This rule was not intended as a further restriction on food, but to protect the reputation of the Community, and to avoid criticisms from lay people. Monks living in dangerous forests were not allowed to accept food from a stranger (*Pāṭidesanīya* 4, Vin IV 181); this rule was intended to protect their health and ensure their safety. (As there were no forest-dwelling nuns, the *Pātimokkha* does not apply this rule to them.)

RESTRICTIONS ON THE CONSUMPTION OF FOOD: (II) ADVICE

The Buddha did not want to restrict his disciples' diet too harshly. An inadequate diet would have been inconsistent with his "Middle Way." We know that Gotama practised extreme ascetic self-mortification before his Enlightenment, when he reduced his intake of food to the point of near-starvation (M I 246). He realized that traditional asceticism and self-mortification did not produce the desired result, and he went back to eating normal and adequate quantities of food. After his Enlightenment, he gave his disciples the following advice: an inadequate diet is one form of excess, and gluttony is another.

When disciples arrived from afar to visit the Buddha, after the Rainy Season Retreat, he would always ask them if they had eaten enough and if they had had problems receiving alms (Vin I 158, 253, 351; M I 206, III 155–156). This simple example shows how broad-minded was the Master's concern for the nourishment and physical health of his disciples: without adequate nourishment it is not possible to practice the religious life. On the other hand, he did not encourage gluttony: on the contrary, he always criticized it. He upbraided the monk Upananda (Vin II 165) and the nun Sundarī-Nandā (Vin IV 211–212) for being greedy. Gluttony, like any other desire, was considered an obstacle to inner progress. Monks and nuns were to try and renounce all thoughts of gluttony, and to avoid even talking about food with others, as such talk constituted "vulgar talk" (A V 127–130). The Buddha taught a gradual path in the *Nikaya* texts, as when he spoke to the Brahmin Gaṇaka-Moggallāna of the need to control gluttony:

> Brahmin, as soon as a monk is able to control his senses, the Tathāgata leads him further still: now, monk, be moderate in your eating. Concentrate and be attentive when you eat: do not eat for pleasure or enjoyment, nor in order to be handsome and attractive; eat only to keep your body going, to protect it from harm, for the benefit of the religious life (M III 2; A II 40, III 388).

So monks and nuns had to be content with little food: just enough to keep their body going. They were to take food from villages and towns as bees take nectar from flowers without damaging them (Dhp 49). This advice was also given for the sake of lay society. If members of the Community had been constantly trying to find food, and if they had eaten more than once a day, it would have been more difficult for benefactors to support them. According to several sermons by the Buddha, the subsistence of monks and nuns was not to be a burden on lay society. In general, the Buddha's disciples were known to eat and sleep little (Dhp-a III 321). Copious meals induce heavy sleep; they are obstacles on the path of renunciation as they prevent meditation, mindfulness and inner progress. To practice contemplation, to be able to meditate for long periods of time without feeling sleepy, and to stay in good health, renouncers had to restrict their eating. However, the canonical texts do not specify in detail the precise quantities of food prescribed for monks and nuns.

Alcohol and Other Beverages

Monks and nuns were not allowed to drink alcohol, or any fermented spirits (*Pācittiya* rule 51, Vin IV 110, nuns' *Pācittiya* 132). Among the ten precepts taken by novices, and the five taken by lay followers, the fifth enjoins abstinence from liquor which causes intoxication and heedlessness (Vin I 83). The code of monastic discipline made the absolute prohibition of alcohol quite explicit. However, when a monk prepared a medicinal drink for a fellow monk who was ill, he was allowed to add alcohol if necessary; but if he happened to put in too much alcohol, it was no longer good to drink, and had to be used as an ointment (Vin I 205). No other kinds of beverage posed any serious problem. Monks and nuns were allowed to drink even in the afternoon. A long list from the *Mahāvagga* (Vin I 246) details permissible drinks: juice made from the leaves, flowers, and fruit of plants, but excepting juices extracted from vegetables, wheat, liquorice and sugar cane.

Medicines

In the *Vinaya,* many amendments to the rules concerned illness. The following rules and precepts could all be transgressed in case of illness: *Pācittiya* rules 31, 32, 33, 39, 47 and 56 and *Pāṭidesanīya* rule 3 for monks; *Pācittiya* rules 84, 85, 117, 118, 128 and 137 and eight *Pāṭidesanīya* rules for nuns; and the precepts of good behavior (*sekhiyā dhammā*) 37, 73, 74 and 75 for both monks and nuns. In the *Vinaya* the health of monks and nuns was given priority over rules concerning food. For health reasons, monks and nuns were allowed to consume medicinal foods. One day in autumn, the master saw some emaciated and unhealthy looking monks. He told them:

> Monks, there are five kinds of food, ghee (clarified melted butter), fresh butter, sesame oil, honey and molasses, which everyone regards as medicines. Although they are nutritious, they do not count as real meals. I permit you to accept these five medicines and to consume them, during "the right time" (Vin I 199).

A few days later, the Master himself amended his permission: "monks, I also allow you to accept the five medicines and to consume them outside the right time." Following this amendment, monks and nuns were allowed to eat ghee, honey, etc. even in the afternoon.

A long chapter from the *Mahāvagga,* entitled *Bhesajjakkhandhaka,* is entirely devoted to illness and medicines. The medicines listed in it were prepared with herbs, roots, fruit, leaves, etc. All kinds of fruit, salt, root, oil and ointment, as well as the utensils necessary for their preparation were permitted. Monks and nuns who were ill were allowed to take these medicines even outside "the right time."

Endnotes

1. In Canonical texts, the Buddha always used the term *bhikkhu* for monks, and *bhikkhunī* for nuns. It seems that these terms were used only by the Buddha. Among monks, inferiors addressed superiors by the term *bhante,* "venerable one," and superiors called their inferiors *āvuso,* "brother" or "friend." Superiority and inferiority here are based on the date of entry into the Community, without distinction of caste, age or level of inner progress. Monks called nuns *bhaginī,* "sister," while nuns called each other *ayyā,* "noble one," or sometimes *bhaginī.* On the other hand, among lay the Buddha's disciples were known as *samaṇā sakyaputtiyā,* "ascetics [*religieux:* see p. 16 note 1], *sons of the Sākyans;*" in some passages from the *Vinaya* texts nuns are called *samaṇiyo sakyadhītarā,* "ascetics, daughters of the Sākyans."
2. This is also true in Jainism, where the term *bhikkhu* is not used to denote simply a religious mendicant, but rather someone who aspires to deliverance.
3. According to the *Cullavagga* (Vin II 300), during the Second Buddhist Council, held at Vesāli, the Elders condemned even the practice of keeping salt on a journey.
4. The category of "soft food" ' (*bhojanīya*) includes various cereal preparations, fish and meat; "hard food" (*khādanīya*) includes roots, tubers, nuts and pastries.

Chapter 5

Money

Indeed, sirs, when Gotama left home to embrace the religious life he renounced everything, silver, gold and all the riches he possessed on earth and underground . . .

(D I 115)

As we have seen, Buddhist monks and nuns did not work to earn their living. They depended completely on lay followers, and so did not need money. In renouncing secular life to embrace the religious life, they also renounced wealth and private property. Given this, did they have any dealings at all with money?

Lay followers provided monks and nuns with robes, food, and other necessities. Some even wanted to give them money to buy things. Were they allowed to accept it? This subject is fully dealt with in the rules of the *Vinaya-piṭaka;* the rules cover three separate areas: monks and nuns were forbidden to accept gold and silver, to engage in trading and to engage in bartering. In the canonical texts, the phrase "gold and silver" (*jātarūparajata*)denotes any monetary unit or means of exchange, as well as the precious metals themselves. The following is the first rule concerning "gold and silver."[1]

> If a monk accepts money, or has someone accept it in his stead, or consents to have it deposited for him, he commits an offense from the *Nissaggiya Pācittiya* category.
>
> (*Nissaggiya Pācittiya* 18, Vin III 237).

This rule was laid down as a consequence of an incident involving the monk Upananda; one day he was going from door to door, begging for food, and a lay follower gave him a few coins of money, which he accepted. Soon afterwards, the same man criticized Upananda; he and some other lay followers said: "Look at these monks, sons of the Sākyans, accepting money just like we lay people." As a result, the Master laid down the rule mentioned above. For nuns, the prohibition is found in the *Nissaggiya Pācittiya* rule 21 from the *Bhikkhunī Pātimokkha.* Even novices were not allowed to accept money (Vin I 83–84).

The other rule concerning money (*Nissaggiya Pācittiya* 10, Vin III 219–223) was also established after an incident involving Upananda, in which he accepted money given by a lay follower in lieu of a robe. Compared to the other rules from the *Pātimokkha,* this one is categorical and precise. The lengthy explanation is receives makes it the most extensive rule in the *Pātimokkha:*

> If a brahmin, a householder, a king or someone from his retinue sends a messenger with money to buy a robe, telling him "Buy a robe with this money and give it to such and such a monk"; and if the messenger addresses the monk in the following words: "Venerable one, this money was sent for the venerable one to buy a robe, may the venerable one accept this money"; then the monk must give the messenger the following answer: "Friend, we do not accept money to buy robes, but we accept a robe if it is given at the right time and if it is suitable."
>
> If the messenger asks the monk "Venerable one, is there a servant I can ask?" the monk who needs a robe must show him a servant, either a servant from the monastery or a lay follower, and say to him: "He is the monks' servant." If the messenger gives instructions to the servant and then comes back to the monk with the following words, "Venerable one, I have given instructions to the man whom the Venerable one pointed out to me as the servant; let the Venerable one approach him at the right time, and he will give him a robe,"

> then when the monk needs a robe, he must go to the servant, and repeat two or three times the following formula: "Friend, I need a robe."
>
> If by repeating this two or three times, he succeeds in getting the robe, it is well. If he does not succeed, he must stand there in silence four, five or six times at most, and if he then succeeds, it is well. If he insists further (more than six times) and succeeds in getting the robe, he commits an offense which entails giving it up as improperly obtained. If he does not succeed in getting it (after six times), he must go himself and see the people who sent him money for a robe, or send a messenger, to tell them: "Friends, the money that you sent to buy a robe for a monk is not being used by that monk. Make good use of your money, and do not waste it." In these circumstances, this is what the monk should do.

The rule can be simply summarized: "you may accept a robe, but you must never accept money to buy it." *Nissaggiya Pācittiya* rule 20 from the *Bhikkhunī Pātimokkha* lays down the same regulation for nuns.

In principle, monks and nuns were allowed to accept material things as long as they were compatible with the monastic life. Several rules from the *Mahāvagga* allowed them, for example, to accept and even to seek what they needed on a journey, to ask robes from lay people provided they were either devotees of the Community or close relatives. But they should never, on the other hand, ask for money or for their favorite food. Only a monk who was ill was allowed to choose his food, but under no circumstances was he allowed to ask for money or to accept it. A story from the *Cullavagga* provides a good illustration of this principle: monks were allowed to ask for the material things which are necessary to build a residence or monastery, but not for money to purchase them. The Master spelled out this rule to a village-chief by the name of Maṇicūḷaka:

> Maṇicūḷaka, I told those who needed grass to look for grass, those who needed wood to look for wood, those who needed transportation to look for transportation, those who needed

an assistant to look for an assistant; but I always told them not to seek nor to accept money under any circumstances.
(Vin II 297)

Regulations of this kind governing how to obtain robes, dwellings, and other material things were typical of the first days of the Community. As the Community expanded and the number of its followers increased, closer relationships were unavoidably formed between monastic and lay disciples. It became necessary to find new solutions and methods to meet the basic needs of the Community, while adapting to changing circumstances; but these solutions were not to upset the Community's ideal of renunciation. We saw in previous chapters how some monks and nuns were appointed by the Community to be responsible for distributing robes, and lodgings. Under new pressures, some lay followers were appointed to help monks in difficult situations. One day, for example, a monk was bitten by a snake; the other monks did not go and get the necessary medicines. The Master then advised monks to appoint themselves a lay helper (Vin I 206, IV 166). The *Mahāvagga* (Vin II 307) says that the venerable Piḷindavaccha was given many monastic attendants by king Bimbisāra. These attendants were householders who lived in their villages with their wives and children.

Kappiya Kāraka

A lay follower who helped the Community with monetary problems was called *Kappiya kāraka*. The *Vinaya* texts specify his responsibilities: to provide for monks according to their needs. He offered his services voluntarily and faithfully to the Community. In that way, monks could feel free to inform him of their needs without any reserve. Moreover, they could trust him and feel confident that he would never make arrangements incompatible with the monastic rules, since he was supposed to know thoroughly what was laid down as suitable and unsuitable for monks and nuns. Thus the *Kappiya kāraka*'s role was especially important in the matter of money. Once, at the great banker Meṇḍaka's suggestion, the Buddha told the monks:

> Monks, some faithful lay followers deposit money with a *Kappiya kāraka* and instruct him in this way: "With this money, provide for the monks according to their needs and in a manner suitable for them." Monks, I allow you to accept what is suitable from the *Kappiya kāraka,* but you must never in any way accept or seek money"
>
> (Vin I 245).

The Master spoke these words as he was going through a forest area, from Bhaddiya to Anguttarāpa with a sizable group of monks. Meṇḍaka convinced him of the advisability of allowing monks to accept the services of a *Kappiya kāraka.* On the strength of this permission, monks could accept things prepared by the *Kappiya kāraka* with the money that lay followers had entrusted to him. The *Kappiya kāraka*'s responsibility and duty towards the Community was to render suitable what was not suitable for monks: lay followers deposited their gift of money with the *Kappiya kāraka* who then took care of everything. Monks did not have any contact, direct or indirect, with the money received and spent by the *Kappiya kāraka,* and in this way avoided involvement with money.

The Prohibition on Trade and Bartering

As we saw above (*Nissaggiya Pācittiya* rule 18, nuns' *Nissaggiya Pācittiya* 21), monks were not allowed to accept money given by lay followers. This rule, however, did not in itself prevent them from engaging in commerce. It seems that some of them took advantage of this fact to do business. People said, "How is it that these monks, sons of the

Sākyans, do business like we lay people?" As a result, the *Nissaggiya Pācittiya* rule 19 (Vin III 239; nuns' *Nissaggiya Pācittiya* 22) was established: it forbade them to engage in any kind of trade, and in dealings with precious metals, ornaments or raw metals.

In addition, *Nissaggiya Pācittiya* rule 20 (Vin III 241; nuns' *Nissaggiya Pācittiya* 23) forbade any kind of bartering. It was established on the occasion of a dispute between Upananda and a wandering religious mendicant (*paribbājaka*). They exchanged some pieces of cloth. A few days later, the *paribbājaka* wanted his piece of cloth back and asked Upananda for it, but Upananda refused. Afterwards, mendicants started to criticize Buddhist monks, and as a result monks and nuns were forbidden to barter.

However, the rule did not forbid monks and nuns to exchange things within the Community. The Buddha himself, as we have seen (pp.48–9) exchanged robes with Mahā-Kassapa. A monk was allowed to accept a robe from a nun, provided he gave her something in exchange, even if it was not worth much (*Nissaggiya Pācittiya* rule 5, Vin III 209). Conversely, a monk was allowed to give a robe to a nun provided she gave him a little something in exchange (*Pācittiya* rule 25, Vin IV 59–60). And when a group of monks was given a valuable blanket, they were allowed to exchange it for something else (Vin II 174). Various other rules from the *Vinaya* provide indirect evidence of the monks' and nuns' right to exchange objects.

The Theravādin Attitude to Money

Although we will not make a general comparison between different Buddhist schools on the subject of monasticism, it will be useful here to go into more detail about the specific attitude of Theravāda Buddhism toward money, as the Theravādins themselves have laid great stress on the issue. *Nissaggiya Pācittiya* rule 18, and the commentary on it incorporated in the *Vinaya* text, embody the Theravādin attitude:

Were a monk to accept money, or to have someone accept it in his stead, or to consent to have it deposited for him, he would be committing an offense from the *Nissaggiya Pācittiya* category. "To consent to have it deposited for him" means the following: if a layman tells him "Let this money be for the Venerable one," and he agrees, the money must be confiscated before (a meeting of) the Community. When money is confiscated in this way, the monk must come before the Community, adjusting his top robe over one shoulder, and he must prostrate himself at the feet of senior monks, bend low, and bowing with clasped hands address the Community in the following words: "Venerable ones, I have accepted money which must be confiscated. I give it to the Community." After giving it, the monk must confess his offense, and his confession must be acknowledged by a competent and experienced monk. The monks must tell a monastery-servant or a lay follower: "Friend, do what you like with this money." If he asks, "What shall I do with it?" he must not be told to buy anything specific, except oil, honey or molasses, which monks are allowed to ask for. Once the money has been used to buy whatever goods are permitted, and once these goods have been brought in, everyone is allowed to make use of them, except the monk who had accepted the money. If it happens this way, all is well. But if the monastery-servant or the lay follower cannot use the money in this way, he must be told: "Friend, take this money away." If he does so, all is well. Otherwise, a monk who possesses the five qualities (he must not behave incorrectly, be unfair out of partiality, hatred, fear, or stupidity, and must know what is and is not to be done) is to be appointed by the Community as a "remover of money." He must remove the money and then throw it away without making any sign (as to where he has put it). If he makes a sign when he throws it away, it constitutes an offense of wrongdoing.

If a monk accepts money, whether knowingly, unknowingly or in doubt (about whether it is really money) he commits an offense from the *Nissaggiya Pācittiya* category. If a monk accepts something he thinks is money, although it is not, or if he is in doubt about it, there is an offense of wrongdoing . . . No offense is committed, however, if he brings money or has it brought inside monastery property or a residence in order to set it aside for someone else. If a monk is mad or is "the first offender,"[2] he is not guilty either.

The position adopted by Theravada Buddhism on the rule quoted above is best understood when it is compared with various interpretations of the same rule by other Buddhist schools. Jacques Gernet[3] gives an excellent account of the different interpretations given by various non-Theravadin schools: the Mahāsaṃghikas are the most liberal, the Sarvāstivādins and the Mūla-Sarvāstivādins give a freer and more open interpretation than the Dharmaguptakas and Mahīśāsakas. On the other hand the prohibition as it is interpreted in the Pali *Vinaya* by Theravāda Buddhism is much more specific, categorical and absolute. The various non-Pali interpretations have it that it is permissible to use improperly obtained money to purchase lodgings, robes, and other things. On the contrary, the Pali *Vinaya* only allows two possibilities for the use of improperly obtained money: either it can be used to purchase some medicinal items (butter excluded), or it must be thrown away. According to the other rules from the *Nissaggiya Pācittiya* category (except rule 22), any improperly obtained object must be given back to the guilty monk after he has given it up to the Community, and has confessed his offense; but this does not apply to money, which must never be given back to the guilty monk. Even medicines purchased with the money must not be used by the guilty monk.

Despite the strict interpretation given to *Nissaggiya Pācittiya* Rule 18, quoted at length above, it is clear that the Pali *Vinaya* did not attribute any impurity to physical contact with money. On the other hand, in the interpretation given by the Mahāsaṃghika *Vinaya*, monks are not allowed to touch money with their hands: gold, silver, or money was to be accepted in a bowl specially reserved for this usage, and with hands wrapped in a piece of material (that is, with gloves on). Some monks from Vesāli would only receive money in a large bowl full of water. The approach of the Pali *Vinaya* was in this case completely different. If one admitted that money was unsuitable for the religious life, then the question did not arise whether it was right or wrong to touch it; "touching money" did not constitute an offense. Pali texts forbade "accepting money" (Vin III 237), whether monks touched it or not. According to the Pali *Vinaya-piṭaka* and its commentary, the Buddha did not impute any magical power, nor any intrinsic impurity to money. From a religious point of view, if money was impure, its impurity concerned the mind rather than the body: it hindered simplicity, non-attachment and renunciation.

There is among brahmins, both past and present, a well-known tendency to abstain from touching certain things defined as impure. In their opinion, whoever touches something "impure" becomes himself impure. Many Brahmanical rituals of purification are based on this notion, which provides part of the foundation of untouchability in ancient and modern India. However, untouchability in India does not only prohibit physical contact with pariahs, but also any kind of relationship with them. We do not know for certain if monks from the Mahāsaṃghika and other schools were influenced by brahmanical notions in their attitude to money. Did they regard money as untouchable because of its impurity? If so, why did they not renounce money altogether? In Buddhism purity and impurity are not concepts which apply at the material, physical and external level. On the contrary, purity is always expounded as an internal virtue related to the mind (M I 36–40; S I 165, 182–183; A V 263–268; Sn 251; Thī 236–251). So there is no reason to believe that money is untouchable and impure for the human body.

According to *Nissaggiya Pācittiya* rule 18 (nuns' *Nissaggiya Pācittiya* 21) as interpreted by the Pali *Vinaya-piṭaka,* monks and nuns were allowed to touch gold and silver; they were not advised, for example to wear gloves or anything of the sort in order to remove money. They were specifically allowed to pick up any valuable objects lying around in the monastery, such as jewels, or to have them picked up, on the condition that they put them aside until their rightful owner recovered them (*Pācittiya* rule 84, Vin IV 162, nuns' *Pācittiya* 161).

Let us look at a significant episode described in the *Cullavagga* (Vin II 294ff.). The incident took place a hundred years after the Buddha's death, on the day of the full moon (*uposatha*), on which lay followers would come to the monastery to take part in religious ceremonies. On that day, the venerable Kākaṇḍakāputta Yasa, visiting a monastery at Vesāli, was astonished at the behavior of the monks: they had placed a large copper pot filled with water in the center of one of their groups, and they were saying to lay followers who had come to visit the monastery: "Friends, give the Community one *kahāpaṇa* or a half-*kahāpaṇa*, one *pāda* or one *māsaka*. The Community could use it to buy various things." *Kahāpaṇa, pāda* and *māsaka* were coins or weights of gold, silver, or copper. What is striking about the incident is the manner in which the monks accepted these coins; it seems that they did not want to touch them. They used a pot filled with water, presumably intending in this way to get money without violating the rule, without accepting it directly from the hands of lay followers. They probably thought that money was untouchable but usable. Whatever their reasons and motivations, these monks acted as real "beggars." The text alleges, furthermore, that the custom dated from a long time before the venerable Yasa visited the town of Vesāli. For a long time monks in Vesāli had been asking lay followers for money, accepting it and using it to purchase various things, and laypeople there had been in the habit of giving it.

One cannot overlook the fact that these monks did need an income. As the Community spread out, new needs arose, related to social, climatic and other conditions. Notably, those monks who traveled to various towns far from their country of origin in order to propagate the Doctrine, needed money if they were to survive in places where there were too few lay followers. Money was probably essential to pay boatfares across rivers and to buy a few indispensable objects. Maybe they used gold, silver, or money, as is shown in the Mahīśāsaka *Vinaya*, "for the sake of activities regarding the Buddha" (Gernet op.cit). But the important question here is whether or not asking for money was consistent with the *Vinaya*.

The custom adopted by the monks in Vesāli greatly upset the venerable Yasa, who was the Theravādin spokesman. In his opinion, these monks were doing wrong, and he publicly objected to it. At first, he addressed the lay followers in Vesāli:

> Friends, do not give *kahāpaṇa*, half-*kahāpaṇa*, *pāda* or *māsaka* to the Community. Money is not permitted to monks, sons of the Sākyans; they do not consent to accept money, nor to ask for it. The monks, sons of the Sākyans, have renounced their jewelry, gold, and precious stones, and they have no money.

Despite the venerable Yasa's advice, lay followers from Vesāli continued to give money to the monks; they were probably unwilling to give up their custom at the command of a monk who was a stranger to them.

Moreover, the monks from Vesāli did not stop at asking and accepting money; they would distribute what money they had obtained among all the members of the local Community. They allotted shares out of the money received on the day of the full moon and gave a share to Yasa, who immediately refused it in the following words: "No, venerable ones, I do not need money. I must not to accept money." The monks from Vesāli were angry at this and ordered Yasa, as a punishment, to ask lay followers publicly for forgiveness.[4] These monks, it seems, were confident that it was correct to accept money. Yasa obeyed their command; but instead of asking for forgiveness, he defended his position by referring to the Buddha's words. According to Yasa, the Buddha had clearly specified his opinion about money in three places: first before a gathering of monks, second to a village chief called Maṇicūḷaka, and finally on the occasion of Upananda's accepting money instead of food:

(i) One day the Buddha, preaching to monks, compared the four obstacles to the religious life to four ways for sunlight and moonlight to be obscured. Sunlight and moonlight, he said, were threatened by clouds, by fog, by thick black smoke and by eclipses. Similarly, the religious life was threatened by four obstacles: alcohol, sexual relationships, money and improper livelihood. A single one of these four obstacles was enough to obscure and destroy the religious life (Vin II 296; A II 53).

(ii) There had been a controversy between some lay followers from the town of Rājagaha and a village chief called Maṇicūḷaka. Everyone apart from Maṇicūḷaka believed that monks had the right to accept gold and money. The dispute was left unsolved. Maṇicūḷaka then visited the Buddha, who confirmed that he was in the right:

> Of course, Maṇicūḷaka, your opinion is absolutely correct. Money is not permitted to monks, sons of the Sākyans; they are not allowed to accept it nor to keep it. They are men who have given up jewels, gold, and precious stones. They do not possess money. If money were permitted, then the pleasures of the five senses would equally be permitted. Whoever is allowed the pleasures of the five senses does not, as you well know, lead an ascetic life, nor the life of the sons of the Sākyans. (Vin II 297).

(iii) Finally, there was the incident involving Upananda, which led the Buddha to establish *Nissaggiya Pācittiya* rule 18 discussed above.

Yasa succeeded in convincing the lay followers, but the monks from Vesāli unyieldingly stood their ground. They produced explanations as to why it was right and legitimate to accept money. This controversy brought about the second Buddhist Council. According to the account of this Council in the Pali *Vinaya,* despite strong opposition from the monks from Vesāli, the senior monks condemned their custom. In the opinion of the latter, accepting and using money was in absolute contradiction to the Doctrine and the Discipline preached by the Master.

Leaving aside the various interpretations by different Buddhist schools, one thing is certain: Theravādins were concerned with this issue. Although rules concerning money were relatively few in number, the strictness of the Theravāda interpretation is shown by the fact that the Pali *Vinaya* preserves a detailed account of the council at Vesāli, along with their interpretation of it. The four rules dealing with this matter are clear: not only is trade forbidden, but also the use of money to purchase clothes, food, and other things. In the Theravādin view, monks and nuns did not have the right to buy anything; they were to rely entirely on lay people for the material aspect of their lives: as long as there were lay followers, monks and nuns did not need money.

Money symbolizes the whole range of material values. If someone accepts or possesses money, his or her renunciation is not complete: his or her life is not yet detached from the the world. This is the reason why the *Vinaya* prohibited money, "gold and silver," even in cases which had nothing to do with commerce. For example, monks and nuns were not allowed to own or use utensils made of gold to prepare medicines (Vin I 203). Of course, the begging-bowl could not be made of gold (Vin II 112–114). These four rules were laid down to counter any temptation in monks and nuns to fall into habits incompatible with renunciation, and to encourage them always to lead a simply life, in a position of dependency on lay followers.

Endnotes

1. [Hereafter, we translate this term simply as "money."]
2. "The first offender" (*ādikammika*) refers to the person whose offense caused the rule to be laid down. The proviso applies to every rule in the *Vinaya*.
3. J. Gernet, *Les aspects économiques du bouddhisme dans la société chinoise du Ve au Xe siècle,* Saigon, Ecole francaise d'Extrême-Orient, 1956, pp. 150–151.
4. In Buddhist monastic jurisprudence, this punishment is called *paṭisāranīya kamma*. The procedure requires the guilty monk or nun to ask lay people whom they have offended for forgiveness (see Vin I 49, 330; II 18).

Chapter 6

Chastity

Two extremes are to be avoided by the monk: being attached to sensual pleasure, which is low, vulgar, worldly, ignoble, and comes to no good; and indulging in self-mortification, which is painful, ignoble and comes to no good. . .

(S V 420)

The first step in becoming a monk or a nun is to abandon lay life, which means to leave one's family. Buddhist monasticism led many married persons to renounce their wives or husbands; single men and women renounced the possibility of marriage.

Most of the first sixty disciples who gathered around the Buddha during the first months of the Community had been married, notably Yasa and his friends, and the young men from the Bhaddavaggiya group (Vin I 15–23; see pp.4–5 above). Did the Buddha and his disciples give a bad example to society? In their opinion, embracing the religious life was a good enough reason to renounce their family. In some circles, indeed, renouncing luxury, family life and sensual pleasures were regarded as difficult and heroic acts. Neither Gotama nor Nāthaputta (Jina Mahāvīra) became subject to general recrimination or public criticism, nor did they acquire a bad reputation for having abandoned their wives and children. This does not mean, however, that everyone admired the attitude of the Buddha and his disciples. Canonical texts mention the disapproval expressed by some of the people of the Magadha country, probably by those who were followers of the Brahmins, and by the Brahmins themselves:

> At that time, sons of well-known and distinguished families from the country of Magadha were practicing the religious life under the guidance of the Blessed One. This upset and angered people: "He is on a path which takes away (people's) children, the monk Gotama. He is on a path which makes widows, the monk Gotama. He is on a path which destroys families, the monk Gotama. . .
>
> (Vin I 43)

The Buddha, then, sometimes provoked strong resentment, as he could seem to destroy families by encouraging young people to renounce their marriage and family life. It is important to see why the *Vinaya* mentions this popular grievance. A true law book, the *Vinaya* is not simply a compendium of rules and advice, but is also a case book collecting judgments which have jurisprudential authority. In my opinion, the *Vinaya* mentions this popular reaction in order to suggest to the members of the Community that they should ignore such criticism. On this occasion, the *Vinaya* adds, the Buddha stood his ground in the face of popular disapproval; it did not cause him to forbid monks to have young and married men join the Community. Soon afterwards, women were also allowed to renounce their husbands and enter the Community, on condition that they obtained permission to do so from their parents and husbands.

Renouncing sexual relations was part of renouncing family life. According to the *Vinaya,* most members of the first days of the Community had eliminated all defilements and had no need of rules to govern their behavior. Rules first became necessary as a result of an incident involving a monk called Sudinna Kalandakaputta. This monk had been a wealthy young man. The words of the Buddha had convinced him that lay life was not conducive to inner progress. After many difficulties he obtained his parents' permission to renounce his wife and his wealth and joined the Community. He is described as very diligent, enthusiastic and conscientious in his religious practice. One day, Sudinna was begging at his father's house. His parents told him: "Dear Sudinna, our family is rich; we have substantial resources, a lot of money, many possessions and large reserves of food. Dear Sudinna, is it not possible for you to remain a layman with such a great fortune and still to earn much merit?" Sudinna rejected their proposal. His parents then asked him: "Our family, dear Sudinna, is rich . . . For this reason, dear Sudinna, beget an heir; do not let the Licchavis (political rulers of the Vajji country) take our possessions from us because the family has no heir." This time, Sudinna lacked the courage to reject their proposal. He thought that his parents' wish for an heir was legitimate, their suggestion fair and sensible: they were only asking him to procreate a child who could later inherit their fortune. What was wrong with that? In the end Sudinna accepted their proposal and had sexual intercourse with his former wife, for the sole purpose of making her pregnant. Back in the monastery, however, he felt remorse. He lost weight, became sad, dejected, sallow and depressed. Questioned by fellow monks, he told them what had happened. They told the Buddha about it. After pronouncing a long sermon, the Buddha established the following rule:

> If a monk who has accepted the Discipline, who has not rejected the Discipline and has not pronounced himself unable to continue (with the religious life), has sexual intercourse, even with an animal, he commits an offense entailing defeat.[1] That monk is one who is defeated; he is not in communion.
> (Vin III 23)

The same prohibition is found in greater detail in the *Mahāvagga* (Vin I 96):

> It is prohibited for a monk to have sexual intercourse, even with a female animal. A monk who has sexual intercourse is not a monk anymore, nor a son of the *Sākyans.* As a man who has been beheaded cannot live with only a body, so a monk

> who has had sexual intercourse is not a monk anymore, nor a son of the *Sākyans.*

There are also many passages in the *Nikāya* texts concerning sexual abstinence: the *Sāmaññaphala-sutta* (D I 63) insists on chastity in the religious life; in several places in the *Aṅguttara-nikāya,* in the *Apāyika-vagga* (A I 265–273) and in the *Indriya-vagga* (A II 141–148), there are sermons prohibiting sexual intercourse; according to the *Tevijjā-sutta* (D I 246–247, 250), whoever has sexual intercourse is neither a monk nor a true Brahmin; the *Sutta-nipāta* includes many exhortations to the ascetic ideal, frequently extolling sexual abstinence (Sn 400, 609, 814, 835); and in one of his discourses, the venerable Ānanda explains at length the advantages of sexual abstinence (A II 144).

Some scholars think that the Buddha established the first rule prohibiting sexual intercourse in the Community in order to conform to the other religious systems of the time. It is not the case, however, that every contemporary religious sect regarded chastity as an essential virtue. In some Jain texts, for example, the Ājīvakas are pitied for not keeping chaste. Many ancient ascetics, including the earlier Jains who followed Pārśva, did not take a vow of chastity.[2] The seers (*ṛṣi*) and ascetics (*tāpasa*) mentioned in some legends shared their ascetic life with their wives; we do not know whether they continued their conjugal relations while practicing asceticism. The *Udāna (p.13)* tells an amusing story about a brahmanical wandering ascetic who tried with great difficulty to lead the religious life in the company of his pregnant wife. The Commentaries to the *Dhammapada* (I 270) and to the *Udāna* (p.241) mention some categories of ascetics who maintained a wife and children; their asceticism consisted in living outside society, but with their family. The ascetic Keniya who is mentioned in the *Mahāvagga* (Vin I 244) was a rich Brahmin who became an ascetic in order to protect his wealth. He also kept several families. During the day he acted the part of an ascetic, but spent the night in sensual pleasures (VinA 270, MA III 399). So there were, it seems, ascetics living with their wives at the time of the Buddha. But they constituted exceptions to the more general tendency of the times: those who wanted to follow the path of inner progress were usually advised to avoid sexual intercourse, and relationships with the opposite sex in general. Once, some monks and nuns went outside in the street together; when they saw them, people said: "We go walking with our wives, and here are these monks, sons of the *Sākyans*, who go walking with nuns!" (Vin IV 63) These people thought that monks should avoid the company of women, that they should not even walk in the street with them.

As for nuns, three rules from the *Bhikkhunī-vibhaṅga* dealt with sexuality. The first, *Pārājikā* rule 1 from the *Bhikkhunī Pātimokkha*, forbids nuns to have sexual intercourse; it is exactly similar to the one laid down for monks. The second, *Pārājikā* rule 5, was established after the following incident: one of the great banker Migāra's grandsons had fallen in love with a very beautiful nun called Sundarī Nandā. She would meet him often and soon came to reciprocate his feelings. She tried to fight against this improper friendship, but she was not strong enough to control herself and one day she let the young man have physical contact with her. As a result, nuns were prohibited any physical contact with a man:

> If a nun, filled with desire, willingly holds herself against, rubs up against, embraces, touches, or presses (any part of) the body of a man who is also filled with desire, in between the collar-bone and the knees, then she becomes one who is defeated; she is not in communion.
>
> (Vin IV 213)

The third, *Pārājikā* rule 8, specified:

> If a nun, filled with desire, willingly takes the hand of a man who is also filled with desire, or the edge of his robe, or if she stands close to him, or talks to him, or goes to a rendezvous with him, or if she waits for him to visit, or enters a concealed place (with him), or prepares herself physically (for such acts

and meetings), then she becomes one who is defeated; she is not in communion.

(Vin IV 220–221)

Monks and nuns transgressing the prohibition of sexual intercourse committed the type of offense which involve "defeat" (vis-à-vis the enemy called sensual desire) (*pārājikā dhammā*); *pārājikā* means defeat. No expulsion, punishment, compensation, forgiveness or penitence can atone for offenses of this category, which also prohibited theft, murder, and boasting falsely of superhuman powers. Whoever committed this kind of offense was thereby regarded as having left the Community for ever. There was no possibility of ever being reordained back into the Community. If a monk could not control himself, if he wanted to have sensual pleasures and lead a married life, he had first of all formally to leave the Community. He became a layman again, free to enjoy the pleasures of life as a householder. Then he was not regarded as one who was "defeated" (since before "defeat" he had withdrawn from the battlefield). If one day he wanted to come back into the Community, and take the Minor and Major Ordinations, he could always do so, if and when he could formally be freed from family ties.

The *Bhikkhu-vibhaṅga* devotes close to forty pages to explaining why sexual intercourse was prohibited. Despite the well-known Buddhist tenet of "the Middle Way," Buddhist monasticism seems to have held an extreme position on this issue. Why did it not advise its members to use moderation in their sexual life, as it did in the case of other bodily functions (eating, sleeping, etc.)? The strictness shown here can be explained in two ways: with respect to the rules of the Community, and with respect to doctrine. First, the Community's rules, accepted by all who joined it, did not allow members to have sexual intercourse, because this would change the nature of the organization: *either* it would occur outside marriage, and Buddhism disapproves of this, *or* it would occur within a normal married life, with all its incumbent responsibilities and worries, buying or renting a house, caring for children and bringing them up, managing the family income, and so forth. There would be no more communal and free life: monks and nuns would be ordinary fathers and mothers in monastic dress. Secondly, at the doctrinal level, the aim was to remove everything which impeded inner progress. Monks and nuns trying to achieve selflessness must be detached from all sources of sensual pleasure. On the one hand, sexual relations entail social and familial responsibilities, and the attendant worries are an obstacle to mental concentration. On the other hand, they involve pleasure, so it is natural for the mind to dwell on them often and with delight, until it becomes a mental habit, called "desire." It was in order to avoid this danger that Buddhist monasticism decided to prohibit sexual intercourse completely.

Some rules aimed to eliminate temptation from the life of monks. Their transgression had to be judged by a solemn gathering of the Community (the *Saṅghādisesa* rules: see Chapter 8). Monks were not allowed to ask a woman permission to have sexual intercourse with her (*Saṅghādisesa* 4, Vin III 130), to speak with a woman on obscene or erotic matters (*Saṅghādisesa* 3, Vin III 126), or to touch a woman, even the edge of her clothes, with desire (*Saṅghādisesa* 2, Vin III 118). Accusing a monk of having had sexual relations was also a very serious matter. Should anyone maliciously accuse a monk or a nun of having done so, they committed an offense according to the *Saṅghādisesa* rules 8 and 9 from the *Bhikkhu-vibhaṅga* (Vin III 157–169) and the *Bhikkhunī-vibhaṅga* (Vin IV 237, cf. Vin II 78). Two special rules called *aniyatāpatti* (Vin III 189–193; see Chapter 8) forbade a monk to sit and talk with a woman in a private room behind closed doors, and to sleep in the same room as a woman, in secret and behind closed doors.

In addition to rules established to prevent opportunities for heterosexual relations, the *Vinaya* includes other rules against certain sexual practices, such as masturbation (for monks, *Saṅghādisesa* rule 1, Vin III 109; for nuns, *Pācittiya* rules 3 and 4, Vin IV 259–261, and *Pācittiya* rule 93, Vin IV 342) and homosexuality (*Pācittiya* 31, 32, 90, 91, 92, 93, Vin IV

287–288, 341–34). Monks and nuns were not allowed to have a eunuch (Vin I 84), a hermaphrodite (Vin I 88), or the seducer of a nun (Vin I 84) join the Community. If such people already were in the Community, they had to be expelled. Monks were also prohibited from drawing erotic pictures on the walls of monasteries and residences (Vin II 151) or on their robes (Vin IV 60), or to have such pictures drawn.

The disciplinary code was not only concerned with sexual abstinence; it also tried to restrict relations of friendship between monks or nuns and members of the opposite sex to a certain extent. Monks were not allowed to preach to a woman in private without a third person being present and able to understand what was said (*Pācittiya* rule 7, Vin IV 20). Monks were forbidden to spend a single night in a house where a woman lived, even if there were other people in the house (*Pācittiya* 6, Vin IV 17). *Pācittiya* rules 43, 44, and 45 were established to avoid improper relations of friendship between monks and women during begging-rounds. Monks were not allowed to walk in the street with an unaccompanied woman (*Pācittiya* rule 67), to plan outings or walk in the street with a nun (*Pācittiya* rule 27, Vin IV 63). However, monks were allowed to accompany nuns on the highway by previous agreement if the road was regarded as dangerous. According to *Pācittiya* rule 28, monks and nuns could go on a boat together, even by appointment, provided it was only to cross the river, not for a (long) voyage or the pleasure of a boat-trip (Vin IV 64). Monks were not allowed to stay alone with a nun in a private room behind closed doors (*Pācittiya* rule 30, Vin IV 68), nor to partake of a meal prepared by a nun without the help of some lay people (*Pācittiya* rule 29, Vin IV 66–67).

This tendency to keep monks away from women was not only typical of the *Vinaya*, but of other canonical texts as well. They contain various direct and indirect statements to the effect that women were an obstacle on the path of inner progress, such as the following passage from the *Aṅguttara-nikāya*, a warning uttered on the occasion of a tragic incident in Sāvatthi, when a mother had sexual relations with her own son:

> To tell the truth, woman is a snare set up by *Māra*.[3] It is better for a monk to quarrel with a man carrying a sword than to speak alone with a woman. It is better for a monk to quarrel with a friend than to speak alone with a woman. It is better for a monk to sit next to a dangerous snake than to speak alone with a woman.
>
> (A III 68).

In a long parable from the *Itivuttaka* (p.114), women were compared to monsters and demons. In some texts, they were compared to venomous black snakes (cf.A III 261–262), in others to fire which one must avoid: "A monk is better off embracing a flame than embracing a woman" (A IV 128). In others still they were described as a defiling element on the path of inner progress (S I 37; II 234). Shortly before the Master's death, the venerable Ānanda Thera asked him: "Blessed One, how is one to behave towards women?" The Master answered: "You must avoid their sight, Ānanda." "But what if we do see them, Blessed One! What are we to do then?" The Master answered: "Do not talk to them, Ananda." "But what if we do talk to them, Blessed one?" "Then you must keep a watch on yourself, Ānanda" (D II 141). This story summarizes all the rules and admonitions concerning relations between monks and women found in Pali texts: "If you talk to them, keep a watch on yourself."

One thing is clear. Pali texts did not attempt to provoke general dissatisfaction or disgust with women. Buddhism does not hold that women are impure or inferior. The texts simply reminded monks of the necessity to be watchful in the face of the powerful seduction naturally exerted by women and other attractive things. The venerable Piṇḍola Bhāradvāja, one of the Buddha's greatest disciples, explained in conversation with king Udena that the Buddha had advised monks to perceive women in three ways: "He must look upon a woman of his mother's age as a mother, upon a woman of his sister's age as a sister, upon a woman of his daughter's age as a daughter" (S IV 110).

Buddhist monasticism has always criticized improper relationships with laity because they offer opportunities to come into contact with women and to get attached to them:

> Monks, there are five disadvantages for a monk who is forever visiting households and spends a lot of time in the company of lay people. What are they? That monk sees women a lot. Seeing them leads to friendship. Friendship leads to intimacy, intimacy leads to love. When the heart is aflame with love, three things can be expected: either the monk lives the religious life without enthusiasm, or he commits a defiling offense, or he gives up the discipline and goes back to an inferior life, to life in the world.
>
> (A III 259).

Rules and admonitions of this kind were intended to protect monks against potential involvements and to warn them of the dangers. Here is another example: as we saw above, a monk was obliged to stay in one place during the rainy season, but if he believed that his religious life was put at risk because of the presence of women there, it was always permissible for him to leave immediately, even before the end of the Rainy Season Retreat (Vin I 150). It sometimes happened that disciples abandoned the path of renunciation and went back to lay life because of a woman, sometimes their former love. A monk called Nanda wanted to go back to the world: he could not chase from his mind the memory of his former fiancée, the princess Janapada-Kalyāṇī, who was a great beauty (Ud p.21, J II 92–94, Dhp-a I 118). On seeing a group of beautiful women, the young monk Vangīsa took fright because of his own weakness; he went to consult the venerable Ānanda Thera without delay, in order to regain control of his thoughts (S I 185, Th-a I 201–202).

In several passages, the Buddha asserted that it was natural for men to be attached to women's physical charms, but detrimental to inner progress:

> Monks, I know of no physical appearance which reduces a man's mind to slavery as does that of women; the minds of men are completely obsessed with women's physical appearance. Monks, I know of no sound which reduces a man's mind to slavery as does the voice of women; the minds of men are completely obsessed with women's voices. Monks I know of no scent which reduces a man's mind to slavery as does the scent of women; the minds of men are completely obsessed with women's scent. Monks I know of no taste which reduces a man's mind to slavery as does the taste of women; the minds of men are completely obsessed with women's taste. Monks I know of no caress which reduces a man's mind to slavery as does the caress of women; the minds of men are completely obsessed with women's caresses.
>
> (A I 1).
>
> Monks, women ensnare the minds of men; whether walking, standing still, sitting, or lying down, whether laughing, talking, singing, or crying, whether sick or even dying, women ensnare the minds of men.
>
> (A III 68)
>
> Monks, women obsess men's minds in eight ways: through their physical appearance, their smile, their talk, their singing, their cries, their behavior, the delicious meals they prepare and through their caresses.
>
> (A IV 196)

These observations, rules and admonitions show to what extent Buddhist monasticism tried to protect monks against the desires and attachments that could be produced or stimulated by the seductive power of women. However, Buddhist monasticism does not present itself as a "mens' shop," where one could only find articles for men. There were also rules and admonitions intended for nuns. To follow the path of inner progress and reach deliverance, women had also to follow the Doctrine; the advice which was suitable for monks was also suitable for nuns.

Nuns were similarly advised to keep away from men and to distrust them. Nuns were forbidden to accept food or drink from a man who desired her (*Saṅghadisesa* rule 5, Vin IV 231; cf.IV 233), or to speak with a man in the dark or in a secluded place (*Pācittiya* rules 11 and 12, Vin IV 268, 269). A nun was not allowed to stand apart alone with a man, even in an open place, or on a main road, a cul-de-sac or at a cross roads (*Pācittiya* rules 13 and 14, Vin IV 270–271). It was an offense to whisper in a man's ear, or to stay in houses in the company of the householders or their sons (*Pācittiya* 36, Vin IV 231–233). A nun was not to be given medicine or treatment by a man for any ailment lower than the navel (*Pācittiya* rule 60, Vin IV 315): "If, without informing the Community or a group of nuns, a nun treats a boil or sore between her knees and her navel with the help of a man, washing it, putting ointment on it, and dressing it, she commits an offense from the *Pācittiya* category." This rule was established as the result of a nun being raped by a man who had come to help her with such treatment. A nun was not allowed to live under the same roof as a man (*Pācittiya* rule 102), to go to a village or cross a river on her own, or spend a night alone away from other nuns (*Pācittiya* 3, Vin IV 226–229); nor to serve food to monks (Vin IV 263), to enter monks'dwellings without permission (*Pācittiya* rule 51, Vin IV 306), nor to sit before a monk without permission (*Pācittiya rule 94, Vin IV 343)*.

There are, nevertheless, fewer rules requiring nuns to keep away from monks in the *Bhikkhunī-vibaṅga* than rules requiring monks to keep away from nuns in the *Bhikkhu-vibhaṅga*. This is understandable, since there were enough rules already laid down in the monks' code of discipline to prevent improper encounters, and there was no need to add extra rules for nuns in order to keep the sexes apart in the Community. As members of the same Community, monks and nuns had in any case to be in contact with each other. Nuns were forbidden to spend the Rainy Season Retreat too far away from monks (*Pācittiya* rule 56, Vin IV 312), or to live in a region where no monks would be staying (Vin II 255, 257). Every fortnight, nuns had to consult monks for the exact date for the *Uposatha* ceremony, and obtain from them the preaching of the Doctrine (Vin IV 314). If a nun was guilty of a serious offense, she had to face disciplinary procedures before a gathering of both monks and nuns (Vin II 255). It was also before such a gathering of the "twofold Community" that nuns were to end their Rainy Season Retreat, and that female postulants had to receive the Major Ordination after two years training (Vin IV 52).

Despite these inevitable contacts between monks and nuns, in general the company of men was thought to be an obstacle on a woman's path of inner progress. The Master uses the same terms, only reversed, which he used for monks in the speech quoted above:

> I know of no physical appearance, . . . sound, . . . scent, . . . taste, . . . and caress which reduce a woman's mind to slavery as those of a man do. The minds of women are completely obsessed with men's physical appearance. . .
>
> (A I 2)

Any attachment, whether on the part of a man or of a woman, was viewed as an obstacle on the path of renunciation. In its concern with the development of their inner life, Buddhist monasticism attempted to keep men away from women as well as women away from men. A look at some psychological advice from the *Visuddhimagga* (p.184) will help us to gain a better understanding of this "partition wall": If a monk goes to a cemetery in order to meditate on the body's impurity, he can choose a corpse as a subject of meditation, as long as it is not a woman's corpse. If a nun goes there to meditate on the body's impurity, she must choose the corpse of a woman. A woman's corpse is unsuitable for a man to meditate upon, and a man's corpse is unsuitable for a woman. They cannot meditate on a corpse from the opposite sex, because it might evoke improper feelings of agitation instead of revulsion (cf. A III 68, IV 42). Monks who start meditating on lovingkindness (*mettā*) must not take the mental picture of a woman as their point of departure; similarly, nuns must not start with the mental picture of a man. A mental picture of the opposite sex might unconsciously stimulate improper carnal love, instead of leading the mind toward lovingkindness.

This kind of practical advice shows how Buddhist monasticism tried to go against the current which naturally carries worldly minds toward the opposite sex and attachment. However, from the doctrinal point of view, sexuality was not restricted to sexual intercourse. Any relationship leading to sensual desire between a man and a woman was described as a "sexual fetter." In the *Methuna-sutta* (A IV 54–56) the Buddha explained to a brahmin the "seven fetters of sexuality":

> Brahmin, there are ascetics and brahmins who pretend to practice chastity, and to this end they do not have sexual intercourse with women. But they consent to be massaged, rubbed, bathed and shampooed by women. They derive pleasure from it, they enjoy and desire it. I think, brahmin, that their chastity is torn, distorted, stained and blemished. These impure men cannot be freed from birth, from old age, from illness and from death. They cannot escape from *dukkha* because they are fettered by sexuality.
>
> Brahmin, there are ascetics and brahmins who pretend to practice chastity, and to this end they avoid sexual intercourse and also being massaged (etc.) by women. But they enjoy themselves with women, they play with them, they laugh with them. They derive pleasure from it, they enjoy and desire it. I think, brahmin, that their chastity is torn, etc. (as above).
>
> Brahmin, there are ascetics and brahmins who pretend to practice chastity, and to this end they avoid sexual intercourse, and being massaged (etc.) by women, and also enjoying themselves with women. But they look at women with desire. They derive pleasure from it, they enjoy it and desire it. I think, brahmin, that their chastity is torn, etc. (as above).
>
> Brahmin, there are ascetics and brahmins who pretend to practice chastity, and to this end they avoid . . . (as above) and they also avoid looking at women. But they remember their smiles, the talks and games that they had with women. They derive pleasure from it, they enjoy and desire it. I think, brahmin, that their chastity is torn, etc. (as above).

> Brahmin, there are ascetics and brahmins who pretend to practice chastity, and to this end they avoid sexual intercourse . . . (as above) . . . and they also avoid remembering women. But they look with envy at householders or at their wealthy sons. They derive pleasure from it, they enjoy and desire it. I think, brahmin, that their chastity is torn, etc. (as above).
>
> Brahmin, there are ascetics and brahmins who pretend to practice chastity, and to this end they avoid sexual intercourse, they avoid being massaged, rubbed, bathed and shampooed by women, they avoid playing with women and looking at them; they do not remember their smiles. . . They do not look at householders or their wealthy sons with envy either. But they practice chastity with the thought that it is a virtue, a ritual and an ascetic practice which will make them be reborn as gods in a future life. I think, brahmin, that their chastity is torn, etc. (as above).

This discourse brings out the fact that, for Buddhist monasticism, abstention from sexual intercourse did not suffice to define chastity; involvement in any kind of sensual pleasure was thought to be a "fetter of sexuality." Sexual intercourse constituted thus only one subsection of "the desire for sensual pleasures." The *Bakkula-sutta* provides another illustration of this idea (M III 126–128). One day the Arahant Bakkula Thera was on his begging round in the town of Rājagaha, when he chanced upon his old friend Kassapa, a naked ascetic. The naked ascetic asked him: "Venerable Bakkula, how long ago did you enter the Community?" The old monk answered: "My friend, I have been in the Community for eighty years now." The naked ascetic asked him: "During these eighty years, how many times did you have sexual intercourse?" The old monk answered him: "My friend, this is not the right question. You must formulate your question as follows: During these eighty years, how many times did the perceptions of sensual pleasures arise in your mind?" Then the naked ascetic asked again: "Venerable Bakkula, during these eighty years, how many times did the perceptions of sensual pleasures arise in your mind?" Bakkula answered: "My friend, during these eighty years, no perception of sensual pleasures arose in my mind." This anecdote shows that Buddhist monasticism addresses the whole issue of desire for sensual pleasures, not just sexual desire. Even in the case of Sudinna, recounted above, the other monks did not ask him why he had had sexual intercourse with his former wife; rather, they asked him:

> Is it not true, brother, that the Doctrine is taught in various ways by the Master in order to eliminate passion, not to stimulate it? Is it not true, brother, that the Doctrine is taught in order to remove fetters, not to create them? Is it not true, brother, that the Doctrine is taught to prevent grasping, not to further it? Brother, the Master teaches the Doctrine in many different ways to uproot the passions.
>
> (Vin III 19-20)

Most sermons to monks and nuns on this subject laid stress on the incompatibility of sensual pleasures with renunciation. When he was explaining the attraction exerted by the five objects of sensual pleasure,[4] the Buddha added: "If someone comes to fall in love with such objects, if he accepts them with open arms, if he tries to grasp them, to secure them, to keep them, then he is caught in a trap. Attachment to sensual pleasures leads to infatuation, and infatuation to slavery" (S IV 60). The objects of sensual pleasures were described as "impediments," the search for sensual pleasures as slavery (D I 72). In the *Mahāsaccaka-sutta* (M I 241) the Buddha declares: "some ascetics and brahmins are slaves to their body; their mind is not rid of desires; they enjoy and feed on desires that they cannot extinguish."

It seems, however, that some among the Master's own disciples did not accept his teaching on the subject of sensual pleasures; they rejected the idea that the objects of sensual pleasures were impediments. The *Alagaddūpama-sutta* (M I 130ff.), for example, was preached because of a monk who did not believe that there was any danger in sensual pleasures. His opinion, that the so-called obstructions (*antarāyikā dhammā*) were not necessarily dangerous, constituted a false interpretation of the Buddha's Doctrine, and a direct challenge to some of his teachings. This monk, called Ariṭṭha, did not hesitate to express his opinion to his fellow monks, who reacted with these words: "Do not speak in this way, brother Ariṭṭha. The Master has elucidated the impediments many times. The Master regards sensual pleasures as real obstacles." But Ariṭṭha did not give up. If the commentary to the *Majjhima-nikāya* is to be trusted, he went so far as to accuse the Master of overstating the importance of the rule prohibiting sexual intercourse, which is the first of the rules whose transgression constitutes an offense entailing "defeat"; Ariṭṭha compared this rule to the doomed effort of someone trying to fence in the ocean. When he refused to change his mind, he was punished by the Community, and the *Pācittiya* rules 68 and 69 were laid down (Vin IV 133–135, 137; nuns' *Pācittiya* 146 and 147). According to the *Bhikkhunī Pātimokkha*, nuns who followed such a monk committed an offense entailing defeat (*Pārājikā* rule 7, Vin IV 218). Novices were not allowed either to take as their mentor a monk professing such wrong ideas; a novice called Khandaka, a pupil of Ariṭṭha, who shared his beliefs, was expelled from the Community (Vin IV 138). Monks and nuns were not allowed to keep such a novice with them (*Pācittiya* rule 70, Vin II 25–26; nuns' *Pācittiya* 148, IV 138).

The Buddha refuted Ariṭṭha's opinion as completely false and dangerous:

> Imagine a man, monks, who wants to catch a snake; he goes and finds a big one, and takes hold of it by its body or by its tail. The snake turns on him and bites his hand, his arm or another part of his body. He dies or suffers mortal agony: he seized the snake in the wrong way. In the same way, monks, some stupid men study the Doctrine, but in studying it they do not wisely reflect on the aim of the teaching. As they do not consider its aim, the teaching does not increase their mental acuteness. They only study the Doctrine in order to criticize it or to refute others in debate. They are not capable of reaching the goal to which the study of the Doctrine should lead. This Doctrine, incorrectly received, will bring them evil

> and suffering for a long time, because they did not approach the teaching in the right manner.
>
> (M I 133–134)

In a second parable from the same discourse, the Master explained that the snake must be seized by the neck to prevent it turning back and biting. In the same way, a wise man must be careful to approach the Doctrine in the right way. Then the Buddha described to Ariṭṭha and the other disciples the disadvantages of sensual desires and pleasures, in a series of ten similes:

1. *A meat bone* with no flesh on it, only some blood: this is given to a dog, but the bone does not satisfy the dog's hunger. Likewise, sensual desires never bring permanent satisfaction.
2. *A piece of meat* for which many birds are fighting: if one bird succeeds in seizing it, he risks dying or suffering deadly wounds from the talons of the other birds. Likewise sensual desires are common to all people; their objects are sought after by all and become the cause of deadly conflicts.
3. *A torch made of straw* carried against the wind: it can severely burn someone who carries it carelessly. If he does not get rid of it immediately, his life in in danger. Likewise sensual desires severely burn the minds of men, and the danger is greater than the one coming from a straw torch.
4. *A pit full of burning coal* to which a man is forcefully led by others: if he cannot break free of their hold by himself, he is sure of being thrown on the fire. Likewise sensual desires are a blaze to which the victim is led by bad company or his own behavior.
5. *A dream of a beautiful landscape* which vanishes on waking up: sensual desires are transitory illusions like dreams vanishing when the dreamers wakes up to reality.
6. *Borrowed things* about which the borrower makes wild boasts in public: likewise sensual desires are short-lived and never become the property of the man who tries to own them and to draw pleasure and vainglory from them.

7. *A tree laden with fruit:* a man who loves fruit climbs in the tree. A second man who cannot climb tries to make the tree fall. If the first man does not climb down immediately, he risks breaking his limbs. Likewise sensual pleasures break all limbs, physical and mental, and bring acute sufferings.

8. *A slaughter-house* (or execution-ground): likewise sensual desires kill the noble part of man and cut off his inner progress.

9. *The point of a sword:* like the point of a sword, sensual desires penetrate deeply and inflict wounds. Unfulfilled or unsatisfied desires and the pains of jealousy are as painful as sword-wounds.

10. *A snake's head:* a man who does not pay attention where he walks will get bitten by a snake. Likewise sensual desires constitute serious dangers for the present and the future.[5]

Another passage explains that sensual pleasures enjoyed in this world now, and those enjoyed in the future beyond death, the perceptions of sensual pleasures enjoyed in this world and of those enjoyed in the future beyond death all belong to the realm of *Māra*. Sensual pleasures lead to greed, hatred and destruction, all things which create obstacles on the disciple's path (M II 261). Canonical texts provide explanations of why sensual desires are harmful and advice on how to uproot them. They lay stress on three things: avoiding the objects of sensual pleasure, controlling the senses and controlling the mind. We read in the *Gaṇaka Moggallāna-sutta* (M III 2):

> Monks, learn to keep watch at the doors of your senses. When you see material shapes, do not get immersed in the general appearance; do not get immersed in the details. If someone lives without controlling his sight, evil thoughts, greed, discouragement . . . find their way into him. So practice control of your sense of sight; keep watch on it, you must have complete control of the sense of sight. . ." (The Buddha then repeats a similar warning for each of the other senses, ears, nose, etc.)

For Buddhist monasticism, renouncing the objects of sensual pleasures and controlling the mind did not suffice to destroy the roots of sensual desire. Meditation (*bhāvanā*) was required to change and develop the mind. Renunciation and self-control are only an aid on the path of meditation.

Endnotes

1. [For an explanation of this term see below pp.144–5.]
2. See A.L.Basham, *History and Doctrine of the Ājīvikas,* London 1951, p.124.
3. *Māra:* literally "death", the personification of all that is evil, of all temptations, of everything that ties an individual to the cycle of rebirth.
4. The five objects (*panca kāma-gunā*), all described as "desired, loved, pleasing, charming, seductive", are appearances (*rūpā*) known by sight, sounds (*saddā*) known by hearing, odors (*ghandā*) known by smell, flavors (*rasā*) known by taste, and tangible things (*phoṭṭhabbā*) known by touch, (cf. A IV 456; M I 175, III 114; S IV 60).
5. This list of ten comparisons is given in brief in the *Alagaddūpama Sutta* (M I 130–142), and elaborated in the *Potalīya Sutta* (M I 359–361) and at other places in the Canon.

Chapter 7

Solitude

> *Monks, take to the road. Travel for the good of the many, for the happiness of the many, out of compassion for the world; travel for the good, the benefit, the happiness of men and gods. Preach the Doctrine. . .*
>
> (Vin I 21)

In the code of discipline of Buddhist monasticism, there is no rule which made solitude obligatory; but in the *Sutta-piṭaka* solitude was thought to provide a suitable and sometimes essential atmosphere for the practice of meditation. To what extent did the practice of solitude remove Buddhist monks and nuns from society? Were they always alone?

The longest eulogy of solitude in the Pali canon is found in the *Khaggavisāna-sutta,* which contains forty-one stanzas (Sn. 34–74). Each stanza ends with the phrase *eko care khaggavisāna-kappo* which means "go alone like the (one horn of a) rhinoceros." The one horn of a rhinoceros symbolizes ascetic solitude. Other images are found in the text: to live alone like "a great elephant staying away from the herd" (Sn 52), to be "like a fish breaking free from the net" (62), to leave "like fire which never comes back to the same place" (62), to go "like a lion whom no noise can frighten" (71), or "like the wind that no net can catch" (71), to live "like a lotus on which water cannot rest" (71). All these images were used to praise the inclination to be alone, with unfailing heart (68), abandoning father and mother (60), forsaking wife and children (38), leaving friends and friendships behind (37, 41), renouncing home and property (44), breaking all ties (45): to be alone like the one horn of a rhinoceros! For one who traveled alone, the *Khaggavisāna-sutta* allowed a companion only if he was intelligent, wise and virtuous (47). In the absence of such a companion, he had to continue alone, "like a king who has given up his kingdom and his country" (46). The same idea, expressed less forcefully, is found in the *Muni-sutta* (Sn 206–220) and in the *Sāriputta-sutta* (Sn 995–975). The Dhammapada (328, 329, 330) compares a solitary to an elephant living alone in the forest.

The *Khaggavisāna-sutta* is obviously not in the same category as other discourses; its stanzas constitute a series of exclamations (*udāna*) about the solitary life. The same ideas are found again and again in several stanzas and the fourth line of each stanza is repeated forty-one times word for word. This *sutta* advocates the solitary life in an exaggerated way; but some scholars have taken it as a standard and have therefore thought that Buddhist monasticism was originally a movement of anchorites. If one takes it as representative of the Buddha's intention, however, difficulties arise: the communal life advocated elsewhere by the Buddha is incompatible with the extreme solitude praised in the *sutta*. How did this praise of extreme solitude find its way into the Canon? According to the commentaries, the *Khaggavisāna-sutta* did not reflect the Buddha's opinion directly, but that of the "solitary buddhas" (*pacceka-buddhā*) who lived many years before the Buddha Gotama appeared.[1] According to this commentary, the Buddha Gotama repeated the stanzas in answer to a question asked by the venerable Ananda Thera about the Enlightenment of "solitary buddhas" (Pj II 46ff.).

Everything that is known about the "solitary buddhas" places them in an essentially pre-buddhist period. No "solitary buddhas" are found at the time when the Buddha's Doctrine is preached and his Discipline practiced. The notion of "solitary buddhas" was not restricted to the commentaries. The *Isigili-sutta* (M III 68–69) lists many of their names, and some others are mentioned in the *Kosala-samyutta* (S II 68–102). In my opinion, this notion implies the remarkable idea that even outside Buddhism, someone can attain the truth. Someone born when the Buddha's teaching did not exist could go into the forest and live as a hermit. Through the practice of meditation and with great effort, he could follow the right path and attain the truth. But as he did not have the power to explain the path that he had followed, he would not become a religious master who could show others the way to *nibbāna*. So a "solitary buddha" was neither a Buddha nor one of his disciples. In the general sense of the term, he was not a Buddhist; but if the term "Buddhism" is used to refer to "the true path," then a "solitary buddha" can be said to be a Buddhist. Of course, according to Buddhism, finding the truth is not a matter of "religion"; what counts is to find and to follow the true path.

The attitude of solitary buddhas towards society, therefore, differed from that of the Buddha and his disciples; they did not attempt to preach the Doctrine or to find disciples, since their knowledge of the Doctrine was not communicable to others. Compared to a flower which grows alone and dies in the forest, the anchorite referred to as a solitary buddha attains knowledge of the truth and dies alone. The attitude described in the *Khaggavisāna-sutta* agrees perfectly with this way of life.

The opinion of the Buddha Gotama on the subject of solitude was different. He practiced complete solitude during his period of self-mortification, a long time before his Enlightenment (M I 79). At that time indeed he probably was like a rhinoceros going his solitary way. He soon realized, however, that complete solitude was excessive; and so, after his Enlightenment, he did not advocate the practice of extreme solitude, but organized a Community. It is true that the Buddha insisted that some monks should go to a forest or to empty places (D II 77; M I 205; A III 343); but he never prescribed perpetual solitude. Canonical texts describe monks who had not reached the stage of Arahant, as well as great disciples and the Buddha himself, living alone at times, or with one, two or a few companions (M I 205, III 263; A III 263; S I 109, II 155, V 12–13, 318; Vin I 350). "Living in a forest" or "in an empty place" meant living away from the crowd, but not necessarily alone. When the Buddha was first invited to spend some time in the town of Sāvatthi, he said to his follower Anāthapiṇḍika: "But householder, *Tathāgatas* (see Glossary) like to live in empty places" (Vin II 158), meaning places away from the crowd. The great monastery that Anāthapiṇḍika had built for the Buddha and his disciples was in fact situated "neither too near the town of Sāvatthi nor too far away from it" (Vin II 159). It is necessary to keep in mind here that the Master's prescriptions were always aimed at particular individuals. Living in a forest might help some monks practice meditation, but not others. When the monk Upāli, for example, expressed a wish to live alone in the forest, the Buddha advised him not to do so. He thought that if Upāli stayed alone in the forest, he could only meditate, whereas if he lived with the great disciples, he could meditate and also learn the Doctrine and the Discipline. Upāli followed the Master's advice and stayed with them (A V 207; Th-a I 370; Mp I 172). In time, he became an expert on the disciplinary rules of the Community (A I 25; Th 249–251) and taught them to other monks (Vin IV 142).

We know that the Buddha rejected Devadatta's proposal that the Community should reside permanently in the forest. He took this opportunity to declare that those who wanted to live in the forest could do so, but those who wanted to choose other places to live could do so as well, as long as these were permissible (Vin II 197). Even monks living in forest dwellings were obliged to stay in contact with other members of their Community and with lay followers. For all these reasons, we must accept the explanation given in the commentary to the *Sutta-nipāta,* according to which the *Khaggavisāna-sutta* was not a sermon emanating directly from the Buddha, but a series of striking stanzas expressing the point of view of the "solitary buddhas."

In order to specify the position of Buddhist monasticism on solitude, we will consider the story of a old monk called Thera, in the *Theranāna-sutta* (S II 282):

> At that time, there lived a solitary monk called Thera, who praised solitude. Alone he would enter the village (for his begging-round), alone he would go back, alone he would meditate while sitting or walking. Some of his fellow monks were surprised by his behavior, and spoke of him to the Buddha, who sent for him. Thera acknowledged that he did live thus in solitude: "it is so, Blessed one. I go into the village alone, I come back alone. Alone I practice sitting and walking meditation. I am indeed a solitary monk, Blessed one, and I praise the life of solitude."

The Buddha neither praised nor criticized him, but said:

> Thera, you do indeed practice one kind of solitude; but I will tell you how to achieve complete solitude. In the solitude that I am talking about, Thera, all that which is past must be relinquished. All which is in the future must be relinquished. Desire and lust in the present must be fully mastered. This is the way, Thera, that the true ideal of solitude can be completely realized. . . The sage who overcomes everything, who knows everything, who is attached to nothing, who is completely free because he has renounced everything, who is without thirst – he is the true sage. This man I call "one who lives alone."

We find an echo of this definition of "true solitude" from the *Theranāma-sutta* in the *Bhaddekaratta-sutta* (M III 187), which means "The Discourse on the devotee of ideal solitude." (cf. *Ānanda-bhaddekaratta-sutta,* M III 190, and *Kaccāna-bhaddekaratta-sutta,* M III 192.) It starts with the following words from the Buddha: "Monks, I will teach you and explain to you what "the devotee of ideal solitude" is. Listen carefully and remember what I tell you." He then explains how to escape from the past and the future: ". . . let him not dwell on the past or pine for the future which has not yet happened. The past is finished. What has not come into being has not yet come to pass. Let him wisely focus on the present as it happens."

These two discourses characterize the genuine ideal of solitude in opposition to a common or everyday concept of it. True solitude is inner solitude; to acquire it, one must relinquish past and future completely, and master desire and thirst in the present. This ideal was also expressed in a threefold classification of "solitude," or *viveka: upadhi-viveka*, "detachment from all possessions or substrates' denoted freedom from all tendencies to rebirth, and so referred to *nibbāna; citta-viveka* was "mental detachment" (from desires); the third, "physical solitude," *kāya-viveka*, "bodily detachment," was meant to help monks and nuns attain the first two.

In popular imagination, solitude consists in staying alone by oneself and for oneself. Similarly, according to some ascetic ideals, peace of mind could only be attained away from the noise of the crowd. A monk whose name Eka-vihāri means "the recluse," declared: "When there is nobody to be seen in front or behind, one experiences the same contentment as one who lives alone in the forest" (Th 537; cf. A III 344). Just as physical solitude is represented in this image of having no one behind or in front, so ideal solitude is characterized by the absence of anxious looks backwards and forwards in time. In both discourses (*Theranāma-sutta* and *Bhaddekaratta-sutta*) the point is this: relinquishing the whole past, one does not turn back, one does not relive the past; giving up all ties to the future, one does not worry about what is to come.

Inner solitude, in which past and future have lost their power to disturb the mind, is compared to physical solitude, in which one is not disturbed by what is behind or what is in front. But it is not enough to free oneself from these two sources of torment, the past and the future, in order to attain the perfect tranquility characteristic of genuine solitude. A third source of torment must be destroyed: deep attachment to any "objects," whether material or simply mental. When in full control of desire and "thirst" in the present moment, one sees things as they really are in the present, with the penetrating knowledge that they are impermanent (*anic-*

ca),unsatisfactory (*dukkha*) and without self (*anattā*). Both discourses agree that the highest level of solitude goes beyond its everyday connotation. We find the same idea in the *Dhammapada (348):*

> Let go of what is in front. Let go of what is behind. Let go also of what is in the middle, and stay above all impermanent existence. Then, with a mind free from all objects, you will never come back to birth or old age.

In another discourse, the *Migajāla-sutta* (S IV 37), the Master gives a definition of the phrases *eka vihāri,* "one who lives alone," and *saddutiya vihāri,* "one who lives with someone else":

> There are, Migajāla, shapes perceived by the eyes: desirable, charming, pleasant, lovely shapes which evoke attractive sensual pleasures. If a monk enjoys these shapes, if he seeks them and gets attached to them, then pleasure arises. Once pleasure has arisen, the monk has ignited his desire. Once he has ignited his desire, he is enslaved. A monk who is chained to the chain of desire, Migajāla, can be called "a monk who lives with someone else."

After providing the same explanation for other objects of sensual pleasures, such as melodious sounds, perfumes, tastes, etc., the Buddha concludes:

> A monk who lives in this way, Migajāla, even if he lives far away from society, in a forest where there is no noise, far from anybody, where he can avoid being disturbed by people, in a place which is proper for monks, even then such a monk can be called "one who lives with someone else."

On the other hand, a genuinely solitary monk is not one who lives physically alone, but one who is not attached to the objects of sensual pleasures, and who frees himself from slavery and the chains of desire:

> A monk who lives thus free from desire, Migajāla, even if he lives in the village, among monks and nuns, among men and women, among kings, royal ministers or members of other religious sects, even then such a monk can be called "one who lives alone," because he has given up desire, his companion.

These sermons lay stress on inner solitude without advocating physical solitude. Physically to withdraw from society is not essential to renunciation. One finds the same idea in the *Anaṅgana-sutta* (M I 30), where the Arahant Sāriputta, the foremost disciple of the Buddha, says:

> A man can live alone in the forest and practice austerities, while still harboring many impure thoughts in his mind; on the other hand, a man can live in a village or a town and practice no austerities, but still his mind can be free of impure thoughts. Of these two, the one who leads a pure life in the village or the town is far superior and more advanced than the one who lives alone in the forest with impure thoughts.

For the Buddha, what matters is not to withdraw from society physically, but to live without attachment, just like the lotus flower (A II 39; S II 140). A sermon from the *Aṅguttara-nikāya* (V 108–111) describes the meditative practice of "disengagement from the whole world" in the following words:

> Ananda, when a monk renounces clinging and attachment to the world, (and) the standpoints, inclinations and tendencies of his mind, and so turns away from things without grasping, then Ananda, this is called the practice of disengagement from the whole world. . .

These various texts show clearly the position held by Buddhist monasticism on the subject of solitude. It was necessary as a preliminary step to leave the quarrels of society in order to follow the path of renunciation and to progress in the contemplative life, but simple separation from society was not a means of attaining detachment. This is why the life of renunciation embraced by Buddhist monks and nuns was not a life devoted to solitude. They were not recluses or independent ascetics, in the literal sense of these terms. It is true that they were not attached to family relations and other ties, but they were not completely isolated either. In practice, as well as in principle, they were not alone.

The Position of Buddhist Monks in Society: (1) The Community

Buddhist monks were essentially social beings, for two reasons. First they were members of a society called *saṅgha* (the Community), in which they had responsibilities, duties and also rights. Second, as we have seen, they depended on lay people for clothing, medicine, and food, and they also had responsibilities, duties and rights in relation to lay society. So they were not isolated, without social relations or friendly contact with their neighbors.

In order to describe more precisely the relationship of Buddhist monks to their Community, we will investigate their admission into the Community, the rules of the Community, and the unity of the Community.

Admission into the Community

According to the texts of the *Vinaya*, the monastic Community came into being with the admission of the first five ascetics. They accepted the Buddha's Teaching and asked to become his disciples. The Master told them: "Come, monks, practice the life of purity to bring a complete end to suffering (*dukkha*)" (Vin I 23). This was the original formula used by the Master in the first days of the Community to bestow the Ordination on monks and nuns. The invitation "Come, monk" brought about immediate and full admission to the Community: in time, admission was separated into two stages, the minor Ordination (*pabbajjā*) preceding the major Ordination (*upasampadā*).

After the second discourse and the ordination of Yasa and his four friends, followed by the ordination of their fifty friends, sixty disciples found themselves "delivered from all defilements," and were sent out by the Master to preach the Doctrine (Vin I 21). This happened a few months after the Buddha's Enlightenment. People from various parts of the country heard their preaching and sought admission into the Community; at first the monks brought them back to the Buddha for ordination. Then the Master allowed monks to bestow the minor and the major Ordinations themselves; but he did not tell them to use the formula quoted above. Now it was the candidate who had to recite a formula, repeating it three times: "I take refuge in the Buddha; I take refuge in the Teaching; I take refuge in the Community" (Vin I 22). However, this second stage in the evolution of the procedures for ordination did not last long.

Following an incident involving an elderly brahmin, the Buddha replaced the formula of the three refuges with a new procedure: henceforth, the Community would only bestow major Ordination on a novice who was presented by his preceptor. No one could enter the Community by himself; everyone seeking membership had to be the novice of a preceptor. It was the preceptor's responsibility to provide preliminary training for his pupil before he joined the Community. The Ordination ceremony was a legal act: a motion had to be put to the Community three times in succession (Vin I 56). A qualified monk would pronounce the following words:

> May the Community hear me! Venerable Ones, this person N. seeks ordination, with the Venerable X. as his preceptor. If the Venerable Ones think it fitting, may the Community give him the Ordination through his preceptor. This is the motion.

He would continue:

> May the Community hear me! Venerable Ones, this person N. seeks ordination, with the Venerable X. as his preceptor. The Community is about to bestow the Ordination on N., with X. as his preceptor. If any of the Venerable Ones accepts the Ordination of N. with preceptor X., let him keep silent. If someone finds it unacceptable, let him speak up.

These words would then be repeated a second and third time; and then the monk would declare:

> N. is ordained with X. as preceptor. This is acceptable to the Community, as the Venerable ones have kept silent. This is the way I understand it.

In addition, the novice had to request the Major Ordination before a gathering of the Community, in the following words:

> I seek ordination from the Community, venerable ones. In compassion for me, may the Community, venerable ones, accept me. Now for the second time I seek Ordination. . . Now for the third time I seek Ordination. . .

The details of this procedure clearly show that from then on the authority, the right and the power to bestow major Ordination rested with the Community. The novice needed to have a preceptor approved by the Community and responsible for preparing him for ordination. He had to be able to answer various questions put to him before a gathering of the Community, when it would be emphasized to him that the occasion called for truthful and correct answers. These questions constituted a kind of oral exam intended to check the novice's physical and mental abilities (Vin I 93).

The number of rules concerning admission into the Community increased with the influx of candidates and the growing complexity both of life inside the Community and of the relationship between the Community and lay society. Many matters were regulated in the *Vinaya*, including the following: the minimum number of monks required to bestow the Ordination, the preceptor's qualifications, duties and responsibilities, the pupil's obligations, the competence and age of the postulants, the probation period imposed on former members of other religious sects when they requested admission into the Community. According to these rules, postulants had to undergo a period of preparation and education under the guidance of their preceptor (Vin I 45). Sometimes this training was given before the minor Ordination, sometimes in between the minor and the major Ordinations. Novices had to wait until they were twenty years of age before they could be given the major Ordination (Vin IV 128–130. Members of other religious sects had to undergo a probation period of at least four months before they could join the Community (Vin I 67).[2]

Monks were not allowed to admit into the Community those who did not possess the requisite qualities. The *Mahāvagga* (Vin I 72–76) includes many people in this category: little children (too small to frighten a crow away), people suffering from leprosy, boils, eczema or epilepsy, soldiers or civil servants who had not legally resigned their office in the service of king or government, thieves, escaped convicts, criminals, people who had undergone punishment by the whip or other methods leaving scars on their body, debtors, slaves, young people who did not have the consent of their parents (Vin I 83), people who had had a hand, an ear, their nose, their fingertips or their toes cut off as a punishment, people inflicted with goitres or elephantiasis, hunchbacks, dwarfs, the seriously ill, the very ugly, those who had lost an eye, the maimed, the crippled, the paralytic, the very old, the blind, the deaf and the mute. Another group of people were debarred from joining the Community or from staying in it: eunuchs, hermaphrodites, those who had murdered their father, their mother or an Arahant, and people who had caused a schism in the Community (Vin I 85–89). According to the *Bhikkhunī-vibhanga* (Vin IV 317–334), several categories of women were barred from receiving the major

Ordination: these included pregnant women, the mothers of unweaned infants, postulants who had not undergone a training period of two years during which they observed the six precepts,[3] postulants who had done so but without having obtained approval from the Community (to do so), rebellious postulants who associated with young men, and those who did not have their parents' or their husband's permission. These lengthy lists show that the Community was not an organization freely open to all who wished to join, although it was always possible to leave it freely and without difficulty. Buddhist monks were thus not isolated individuals, but members of a society with well defined rules of admission. It is possible to get a clearer idea of the qualities required of members of the Community by focusing on the motivation behind its rules.

The Community's Rules

When for the first time the venerable Sāriputta Thera expressed his desire to have a code of rules laid down for the Community, the Master rejected the idea of rules established in the abstract. He was concerned that an abstract Rule would not allow the Community to adapt to changing circumstances (such as the dispersion of its members, excess of material goods or the development of scholarship). Since circumstances were likely to change, it was better to lay down rules as need arose (Vin III 9); so the Master established rules as the occasion demanded, and did not hesitate to revise or amend them when necessary. We have had ample evidence of the fact that the *Vinaya* rules were not simply designed to create a propitious atmosphere for a life free from defilements; they also laid stress on health and comfort, and insisted on the observance of proper social customs inside the Community. They regulated every daily act of the monks, their way of eating, of walking, of dressing, etc, down to small details of behavior. The "rules of good behavior" (*sekhiyā dhammā:* Vin IV 185–206) show to what extent the *Vinaya* texts tried to fashion individuals who were well-adjusted to the customs both of the Community and of lay society.

The rules of the Community were established with ten intentions in mind (Vin III 21; IV 91, 120, 182, 299):

1. Protecting the Community
2. Insuring the Community's comfort
3. Warding off ill-meaning people
4. Helping well-behaved monks and nuns
5. Destroying present defilements
6. Preventing future defilements
7. Benefiting non-followers
8. Increasing the number of followers
9. Establishing the Discipline
10. Observing the rules of restraint.

Eight out of the ten reasons given here deal with the relationship which is to exist between monks inside the Community, as well as between monks and society outside the Community. Only two of these reasons, numbers five and six, specifically concern the individual issue of destroying defilements. The Community's regulations were thus for the most part motivated by the desire to safeguard the place of monks both in the Community and in the wider social and religious environment.

The Unity of the Community

Another aspect of the social nature of Buddhist monasticism deserves our attention: the number of rules and amount of advice concerning unity and unanimity between members of the Community. The Buddha is represented in the canonical texts as laying great stress on unity among his disciples: "the unity of the Community is a happiness, and happy is the life of united monks" (Dhp 194). The *Pātimokkha* (Vin III 172, 175; cf. M III 9–10) exhorts monks to be united: "Members of the Community who live united, in friendship and without disputes, are happy, recite (the disciplinary code) together and live in comfort."

The Community's regulations instituted various ceremonies to strengthen unity among its members. For example, the ceremony of *Uposatha* in which all monks or nuns were requested to participate, took place at the end of every lunar half-month (on the fourteenth or fifteenth day of the lunar month depending on its length), in a special meeting hall (called *uposathāgāra*) in the monastery. The main ritual of this statutory ceremony was the recitation of the disciplinary code (the *Pātimokkha*); members of the Community were thus brought together to reaffirm their unity. The ceremony – in which only those who had received the major Ordination were allowed to participate – provided them with an opportunity to discover and confess any offense which might have been committed. A qualified monk would pronounce the following words:

> May the Community hear me, Venerable ones![4] Today is the day of *Uposatha*, the fifteenth day of the fortnight. If the Community is ready, let the Community perform the ceremony of *Uposatha*, and recite the *Pātimokkha*. What is the Community to do first? It must recite the declaration of purity. I will recite the *Pātimokkha*. Let all of us here listen and pay attention.
>
> Whoever has committed an offense must declare it. Whoever is without fault must keep silent. From your silence, Venerable ones, I will infer that you are pure. Just as a single man must answer a question addressed to him, so it is in this gathering, when the question has been repeated three times. A monk who does not confess an offense which he has committed and which he remembers, once the question has been asked three times, is guilty of deliberate lying. And deliberate lying, Venerable ones, is a hindrance to the religious life. Such are the words of the Master. This is why a monk who has committed an offense, who remembers it and is intent on purification, must declare his offense; for when it is revealed there comes to be comfort for him.

In fact, the ceremony was not a simple recitation. Monks and nuns were actually requested to undertake a thorough self-examination. We can say that the ceremony was a kind of "quality control" for the Community. A monk appointed by the Community would recite or read out the disciplinary code. At the end of every set of rules, he would ask the monks or nuns:

> Venerable ones, I have just recited this set of rules. I ask you, in the name of the Community, whether you have transgressed these rules. [He would repeat the question three times, and then continue:] Venerable ones, I infer from your silence, in the name of the Community, that you have not transgressed these rules."

This ceremony gives us a good example of the way monks tried to purify themselves individually while living in community. The *Mahāvagga* (Vin I 112–116) describes the correct or incorrect ways of reciting the disciplinary code, whether in a complete or partial recitation. The speaker had to be a senior monk, and able to speak in a clear enough voice. If no qualified monk was to be found in one monastic district to recite the code, a monk who had just received the major Ordination was sent to another district in order to learn it. If a monk was unable to take part in the *Uposatha* because of illness, he could send his "declaration of purity" through another monk who would proclaim it before the gathered Community (Vin I 121). A monk who was ill could be carried to the ceremony if he wished. If he could not be moved, the local Community had to assemble at his bedside. If a monk was kept away for other reasons, for example if he was held prisoner by soldiers or bandits, other monks were always under the obligation to attempt to secure his release, through friendly negotiations with his captors, so that he could take part in the *Uposatha*.

The *Vinaya* lays great stress on another aspect of the Community's unity: to perform a legal act (*saṅgha-kamma = vinaya-kamma*), it was an absolute necessity that all the members of the Community in one district be present, without exception. Monks were only dispensed from attending if they were seriously ill, physically or mentally. These were the only cases when the local Community could gather in the knowledge that some of its members were missing. Even monks who had attained the highest degree of inner progress had to take part, as is well illustrated in a story from the *Mahāvagga* (Vin I 123). In those days, the Arahant Mahā-Kappina Thera lived alone in the Deer Park near Rājagaha, and wondered to himself: "Am I required to go the the ceremony of *Uposatha?* Am I to go to the statutory ceremonies of the Community or not, since I am completely pure?" Hearing about his disciple's hesitation, the Buddha told him: "Mahā-Kappina, if people like you do not respect the statutory ceremonies of the Community, who will? So go and attend the ceremony of *Uposatha* and the (other) statutory ceremonies of the Community, Mahā-Kappina; do not avoid going."

Concord and harmony between monks was reinforced by the Rainy Season Retreat, during which all monks from the same region would gather as a local Community to perform the *Uposatha* and other statutory ceremonies. Whatever the original motivation behind this custom might have been, the three months retreat soon became a major opportunity for monks to enjoy social life. During this time they were expected to live in harmony and friendship, meditating and discussing the Master's teaching. After the Rainy Season Retreat, they would take to the roads. Once a group of monks from Kosala observed their retreat in a particular way: thinking that silence was a great virtue, they decided on the eve of their retreat to abstain from speaking for the next three months. Afterwards when they visited the Buddha, he asked them if their retreat had been conducted properly and successfully. They answered: "Blessed One, it was very successful. We observed the virtue of silence and remained without speaking for three months: we were very happy." The Buddha did not approve of their behavior:

> Monks, these stupid men spent their time uncomfortably, but they pretended to be very happy. Monks, these stupid men

> spent their time like a flock of sheep, like a bunch of lay-abouts, but they pretended to have a very successful time. Monks, how could these stupid men embrace the practice of silence, in imitation of other religious sects?

The Buddha took this opportunity to forbid vows of silence (Vin I 159). The practice of silence was not permissible, even during the Rainy Season Retreat, because it was thought to be an obstacle to monks' unity. According to a permission expressly given in the *Mahāvagga* (Vin I 142), for example, if a monk received a message from another monk, a nun or a novice, who were losing heart in the practice of the religious life, they had to leave immediately to see this person and give him or her advice, even during the Rainy Season Retreat.

The end of the Rainy Season Retreat was marked by two important ceremonies: the *pavāraṇā*, which only involved monks, and the *kaṭhina*, which we described earlier. The *pavāraṇā*, at which each monk asked the others to reproach him publicly for any misdeed he might have committed during the retreat, was intended to enhance harmony between the members of the Community. Monks would assemble in a solemn gathering, and each one of them, sitting on the floor in an attitude of respect, and raising his clasped hands, would address his fellow monks in the following words:

> I beseech you, Venerable ones of the Community, if you have heard of something reprehensible in my behavior, or have perceived it, or if you entertain any suspicion against me, take pity on me, Venerable ones, and tell me. If I recognize it, I will want to confess it.

The tenth section of the *Mahāvagga* (Vin I 336–358) and the seventh one of the *Cullavagga* (Vin II 179–204) list the advice and rules aimed at preventing schisms in the Community (*saṅgha-bheda*). Verbal disputes would arise from time to time on matters of discipline or doctrine. A group of monks in

Kosambi disagreed about a problem of discipline, and the dispute went very far. However the monks soon managed to come to an agreement and then went to visit the Buddha, who took this opportunity to explain to them how to live in harmony with each other, and how theoretical problems concerning the Doctrine or the Discipline should be resolved without dispute or schism (Vin I 352, II 156; cf. D II 125, M I 320–325, II 238–243, It 11–12). Provoking a schism was regarded as a major offense, in the same category as killing one's mother, one's father or an Arahant, or wounding a Buddha (Vin II 193). Monks and nuns were not allowed to attempt to provoke a schism, nor to harbor opinions liable to lead to a schism (*Saṅghādisesa* rules 10 and 11 in the *Bhikkhu-Pātimokkha*, 14 and 15 in the *Bhikkhuni-Pātimokkha*). Should a monk hear about some monks or nuns somewhere attempting to provoke a schism, he was allowed, even during the Rainy Season Retreat, to go to them and give them advice so as to restore unity (Vin I 151).

When groups of disciples came to visit him, the Buddha would ask them if they had enough food, if they were happy with the way they had spent their time, and if they lived together in harmony: "I hope that you are on friendly terms with everyone, monks, that you live in harmony like milk and water (mixed), looking upon each other with eyes of affection" (Vin I 158, III 156). The *Mahāvagga* speaks in the same way of monks living together: "They lived in harmony, like milk and water, looked upon each other with eyes of affection, with respect and mutual consideration; they had different bodies but one mind" (Vin I 351, cf. M I 206). It was each monk's duty to be polite and considerate toward his fellow monks (D III 245, M I 33, cf. M I 322, A III 289). Lack of friendly feelings towards fellow monks was thought to be an obstacle on the path of inner progress (M I 101–104).

In conclusion, let us repeat, Buddhist monks and nuns were not isolated individuals; they lived as members of their own societies, the *Bhikkhu-* and *Bhikkunī-saṅgha*, with detailed regulations designed to insure proper behavior and well-being.

The Position of Buddhist Monks in Society: (ii) Relations with Laity

Buddhist monks and nuns may seem to have been radically cut off from lay society, because of their attitudes, customs and behavior. Their way of life was in one sense completely different from that of lay people, and they remained on the margins of the world's affairs. But in religious matters, they were very close to lay people, in three different ways: they depended on them for their subsistence, they encouraged their faith and support by providing examples of good behavior, and they acted as their religious advisers.

The Dependence of Monks on Lay People

As we have emphasized repeatedly, Buddhist monks and nuns relied on lay followers for food, clothes, lodging and medicine; although they did not take part in social production, they did take part in consumption. Despite these ties to society, however, they were not involved in economic competition, since their needs were so few. Their dependence on laity constituted a stable bridge between the Community and lay society. Lay people contributed to the Community's support, indeed they assumed full responsibility for it, and this gave them the right to criticize monks or nuns who deviated from right conduct.

For their part, monks and nuns were to strive to maintain the high standards of religious life that would make it worthy of respect. Their success in doing so both attracted people to Buddhism, and gave them sufficient status to be able to inflict (non-violent) punishment on lay people who deserved it. Lay people were always free to criticize bad conduct in monks or nuns, but if one of them accused a monk or nun without good reason, the Community was not to let it pass: the punishment consisted in refusing to accept the alms offered by the offender. This was known as "the (formal) act of overturning the bowl": monks would go to the offender's house with their begging-bowls, but in a symbolic gesture they would overturn their bowls to demonstrate that they did not accept anything from this lay person, that in fact the Community refused to admit him or her as a follower.[5] The *Cullavagga* (Vin II 124ff.) recounts the following story: one day a lay follower, prince Licchavi Vaḍḍha, had accused the venerable Dabbamallaputta of having raped his wife. The judgment of the alleged offense revealed that the accuser had incriminated the monk in order to ruin his reputation and have him expelled from the Community. The monks punished Licchavi Vaḍḍha by overturning their bowls, but suspended the punishment after he confessed his offense and publicly asked for forgiveness. According to the *Vinaya*, this punishment could only be inflicted or suspended through a legal act of the Community. The *Cullavagga* text gives a list of cases when this punishment could be inflicted on a lay follower: if he had tried to prevent devotees from offering gifts to monks, if he had tried to harm monks, to drive them away from a residence, to insult them, to sow dissension among them, and to speak ill of the Buddha, his Teaching and the Community. This custom provides a good illustration of the relation between monks and lay people, at least in some provinces: if lay society and the Community had not had close and lasting religious relations, such a punishment would not have been possible. But this same punishment allowed monks to set limits to their dependence on lay people: if some lay people were not suitable followers, the Community refused to rely on them. Being excluded in this way was thought to be very much to the disadvantage of the people concerned, and this is the reason why Licchavi Vaḍḍha came before the Community to ask publicly for forgiveness (Vin II 124–127).

Monks' and nuns' dependence on lay people acted as a guarantee that the relationship between the Community and lay society would endure, through their exemplary conduct and the laity's faithful support. Buddhist lay followers had the duty and responsibility to support the Community. For their part monks and nuns had the duty to help lay people remain faithful to the Three Jewels by setting examples of good behavior.

Encouraging the Faith of Lay People

The Buddha's teaching spread thanks to the exemplary conduct of his disciples. Every day they went from door to door or in the streets, providing living examples of how to practice the Master's teaching. On seeing a Buddhist monk for the first time, a wandering brahmanical ascetic asked him: "Friend, your composure is perfectly serene; and your skin is perfectly pure and bright. Friend, why did you leave family life? Who is your Master? Whose Doctrine do you follow?" (Vin I 39). Many people were said to have been attracted to the new religion because of the good behavior of members of the Community. But there were also many people who were dissatisfied with the behavior of certain disciples. The Master often took into consideration the criticisms and proposals emanating from lay people. The *Vinaya* indicates clearly that most of the rules established in the disciplinary code conformed to the social and religious customs of the time. When a monk or a nun misbehaved, the Master would remind them: "This is not a thing to do. This is not the way, monks, to persuade non-believers; they will be dissuaded and believers will turn away." In other words, the behavior of monks and nuns was to "bring satisfaction to non-believers and cause the number of believers to increase" (*appasannānaṃ pasādāya, pasannānaṃ bhiyyobhāvāya*); this phrase is repeated in 409 places in the *Bhikkhu-vibhaṅga* and in the *Bhikkhunī-vibhaṅga*.

It is easy to understand the reason for this; good behavior is favorable not only to a monk's own well-being, but also to the happiness and well-being of many others. This is why the *Dhammapada* (382) says that "even a young novice who devotes his life to the Doctrine of the Great Enlightened One lights up this world like the moon coming out of from behind the clouds."[6] It is not our intent here to decide whether such a monk really "lights up" society or not; in the perspective of this study, what matters is the *idea* that the religious life is not only embraced by monks and nuns, and even by novices, for their own well-being, but also for the inspiration and religious benefit of others.

While it was the duty of monks and nuns to edify non-believers and to increase the number of believers by setting a good example, precautions were taken in the *Vinaya* to avoid hypocrisy. In the *Nikāya* texts also, a frequently recurring passage condemns deception, coaxing, insinuation and greed as forms of "improper livelihood" (e.g., M III 75). They were not allowed to make a show of their virtues in order to gain new adepts, nor to display their miraculous powers in front of lay people (Vin II 112). They were forbidden to reveal to lay people, and sometimes even to their fellow-monks, that they observed one or another ascetic practice.[7] They were not to boast of any superhuman perfection, nor even simply to say: "I choose to live in solitude," (Vin III 93). These rules were established to fight hypocrisy and prevent monks from taking advantage of lay people.

Monks and nuns had to do all they could, within the bounds of what was proper, in order to improve the religious devotion of lay followers. According to the regulation laid down in the *Mahāvagga* (Vin I 139), if a monk received the following message from a lay person, "Come, venerable one, we wish to hear the Doctrine," or "Come venerable one, we have built a residence, and we wish to give it to the Community and to hear the Doctrine," he had to grant the request even during the Rainy Season Retreat. Monks and nuns were expected not to neglect the religious needs of lay people, and had a duty to encourage them to remain faithful. On the other hand, we must not forget that they were not allowed to have improper relationships with lay people, or to become too close to them (*Saṅghādisesa rules 13* from the *Bhikkhu Pātimokkha* and 12 from the *Bhikkhunī Pātimokkha*). Nuns were forbidden to help with the cooking or the housework in lay households (*Pācittiya* rules 36 and 44, Vin IV 293–294, 299–300).

The Role of Religious Adviser

The essential feature of the Community's relationship to lay society was the obligation to preach and teach the Doctrine. Lay people supported the Community through gifts of food and clothes, and in exchange monks and nuns showed them the right path. The Master explained the solidarity between the material gifts (*āmisa dāna*) of lay people and the spiritual gifts (*dhamma dāna*) of monks in the following words:

> Monks, householders and brahmins are very helpful to you, since they give you robes, food, lodging, medicine and treatment when you are ill. You too, monks, are very helpful to householders and brahmins, since you teach them the Doctrine."
>
> (It 111–112)

The duty of monks to teach the Doctrine goes back to the first days of the Community; as is recounted in a well-known passage from the *Mahāvagga* (Vin I 21), the Buddha told his disciples, a few months after his Enlightenment:

> Monks, I am free of all ties, human and divine, and so are you, monks, free from all ties, human and divine. Monks, take to the road. Travel for the good of the many, for the happiness of the many, out of compassion for the world; travel for the good, the benefit, the happiness of men and gods. Preach the Doctrine. . .
>
> (Vin I 21)

From the first, the Buddha's teaching was a message openly addressed to all; disciples traveled in order to spread it. Lay people relied on monks to preach the Doctrine and sometimes came to the monastery to hear them preach; if monks did not preach they were upset. Once, probably in the first days of the Community, a few monks who greatly admired the virtue of silence gathered together in the monastery on the day of the *Uposatha*. Lay followers came to hear the Doctrine, but the monks remained silent in front of their audience. The people were upset and reproached the monks for behaving like "dumb" pigs.[8] When he heard about it, the Master advised monks gathered on the day of the *Uposatha* to preach the Doctrine to lay followers rather than to remain like "dumb pigs" (Vin I 101). Even the begging-round was sometimes part of the "proselytizing campaign" of Buddhist monks. A monk would approach someone he did not know to ask him for alms; although he did not speak to him, the two would gradually come to know each other, and their acquaintance paved the way to discussions of the Doctrine. The Buddha would sometimes beg at the house of very unsympathetic brahmins. They received him with hostility, but he would still take the opportunity to deliver some great sermon (cf. S I 165, 167, 171ff., Sn p. 12ff). Despite the difficulties they encountered in some places, monks did not hesitate to go there in order to convert people. They acted "in the interest and for the happiness of the many." The *Itivuttaka* (p. 108) has many epithets for such preachers: masters, leaders of caravans, destroyers of passions, dispellers of darkness, bringers of light and brightness, torchbearers, enlighteners; they could also be called "Aryans" (noble ones) or "Munis." (In non-Buddhist use, the term *muni* means a "Silent Sage," but for Buddhism "one does not become a sage simply because of a vow of silence," Dhp 268). The Buddha wished expressly that even elderly disciples should take part in the teaching of the Doctrine. The Arahant Mahā-Kappina Thera was in the habit of staying alone, enjoying the bliss of deliverance, but the Buddha sent him to preach the Doctrine to his fellow-monks. He later became the most famous disciple to give advice to monks (A I 25).

According to the canonical texts, several nuns were renowned for their wisdom and their skill at preaching the Doctrine. Once the venerable nun Khemā gave a sermon before king Pasenadi, who was so pleased with it that he stood up from his seat and respectfully bowed before her (S IV 374); she is mentioned in canonical texts as the most celebrated of learned nuns (A I 25). Dhammadinnā Therī was renowned as the best preacher among nuns (A I 26). When the Buddha heard the answers she gave to some questions put to her by a lay follower called Visākha, he said: "Visākha, the nun Dhammadinnā is truly wise, she is very learned; if you had put these questions to me, I would have given you the same answers" (M I 304). On another occasion, he praised a sermon delivered by the nun Kajaṅgalā Therī in similar terms (A V 54–56). Canonical texts quote several discourses pronounced by nuns on various occasions (A I 88, II 164, 347, S II 236).

Did all monks and nuns go out to preach? At first, only disciples who were "free from all ties, human or divine," would be sent to preach the Doctrine. Later on, all learned disciples had to take part, except novices, the very elderly, those who were ill, and those who showed no aptitude for teaching: the latter would serve the monastic Community in other ways, like Dabbamallaputta Thera, for example, who was in charge of arrangements for lodging and eating in the monastery at Rājagaha (Vin II 75). Teaching the Doctrine was not easy for everyone. The Arahant Mahā-Kassapa Thera, for example, would not preach often; despite his great wisdom, he was a poor preacher, and one day greatly disappointed some nuns with his sermon (S II 215). Among renowned preachers, some were monks and nuns who had not attained the stage of Arahantship. When Puṇṇa Thera left for Sunāparanta to spread the Doctrine there, he had not yet become an Arahant (M II 267, S IV 60). The venerable Ānanda Thera was also not an Arahant, but he was an excellent preacher; when he delivered the sermon called the *Acchariya-Abbhutadhamma-sutta* (M III 119), the Buddha listened to it and thanked him at the end, as he sometimes did when monks preached (cf.A III 195). It is true that Ānanda, thanks to the closeness of his relationship wit his Master, had an extensive knowledge of the Doctrine; but other monks and nuns who were not Arahants were also renowned as preachers. Nevertheless the Buddha did advise monks and nuns to reach a certain degree of inner progress before preaching to others (A V 10).

Monks and nuns undertook to preach the Doctrine; the purity of their behavior and their progress on the path of inner development were not simply intended for their personal benefit. The Buddha expressed this in the *Itivuttaka* (p.111):

> There are three kinds of individual who are born in this world in the interest of the many, for the happiness of the many . . . out of compassion for the world, for the good, the benefit, the happiness of men and gods. Who are these three? A Buddha, his disciple who is an Arahant, and his disciple who is progressing on the path towards Arahantship. These three preach the Doctrine, which is good in the beginning, good in the middle, and good at the end.

Endnotes

1. The *Mahāvastu* (I 357) agrees with this Theravādin view.
2. This obligation applied neither to the Sākyans nor to the Jaṭila ascetics. The Sākyans were considered to be naturally suited, because of their natural affection towards the Buddha and the Community. Jatila ascetics were granted this special privilege because of their belief in *karma,* the moral theory of action and its results.
3. This probationary period, during which they were known as female postulants (*sikkhamānā*), had to be approved by the Community following the same procedure as the one we have just discussed for the Ordination of male novices. After the Community had accepted her, a postulant promised to observe six precepts for two years. These precepts were the five incumbent on all lay Buddhists with the addition of the prohibition on eating after noon, shared with novices, monks and nuns. Rather confusingly, perhaps, both male and female novices (*sāmaṇera, sāmaṇerī*) followed a longer list of ten precepts (see Appendix 3). However, while a male novice could proceed

directly to the major Ordination at any time (provided he was at least twenty years old), a female novice had first to complete this probationary period of two years as a "postulant." (This was one of the eight special conditions imposed on the nuns' Order by the Buddha: see Appendix 1, pp.159–60). The age limit of 20 years to obtain the Major Ordination was a condition also for female postulants who were unmarried (see *Pācittiya* rules 71, 72, 73); but a young woman who had entered into the married life could obtain the Major Ordination if she was already 12 years old (see *Pācittiya* rules 65, 66, 67). For such a candidate the necessary conditions were (i) obtaining permission of her husband, (ii) spending the probationary period of two years, (iii) obtaining the approval of the Nuns' Order.

4. The *Uposatha* ceremony for nuns was held in their own meeting hall, where they were addressed as "noble ladies" (*ayyā*).
5. The Ceylon Chronicles recount that one time the Community of the Mahā-vihāra (in Ceylon) inflicted this punishment on king Dāṭhopatissa II (650–658 A.D.) (cf. *Mahāvamsa,* Chapter 45, 29–31).
6. According to the Ceylon Chronicles, emperor Asoka (268–239 B.C.) became interested in Buddhism after he witnessed the good behavior and serenity of the novice Nigrodha as the latter was walking in front of the royal palace (cf. *Mahāvaṃsa* Chapter V, 21–22).
7. Rigorous ascetic practices and self-mortification are rejected by Buddhism as harmful rather than useful; but a few mild ascetic practices, called *dhutaṅga,* are accepted as suitable to help certain monks or nuns control their inner problems. These *dhutaṅga,* however, are never obligatory in Buddhist monasticism.
8. Canonical texts (e.g. Vin I 159) make ironical use of the phrase *mūgavatta,* "the vow of dumbness," to denote the vow of silence taken by members of other religious sects at the time of the Buddha.

Chapter 8

The rules of the Community

*"Ānanda, some of you might think after my death: "The Master's teaching has come to an end; we have no Master any more." This is not the right way to look at things. The Doctrine (*dhamma*) and the Discipline (*vinaya*) which I have taught and established will be your Master when I have departed from this world. . . Work out your salvation with diligence."*

(D II 154, 156).

Monastic life required that specific practices regarding clothes and lodging, money and food, solitude and inner progress should be observed; this implies, on one hand, training and initiation, and on the other hand, a set of regulations.

The Relationship between Preceptor and Pupil

As we saw in the last chapter, no one could be admitted into the Community without first spending time as a novice under the guidance of a preceptor (*upajjhāya*) whose role it was to give preliminary training to the candidate for admission. A special period of training or probation was required, particularly for former members of other religious sects, and for elderly people, even before entering the Buddhist noviciate. If someone took on the monastic robe without having received the Ordination, he or she could not be regarded as a member of the Community, but as a "usurper" (*theyyasaṃvāsaka*). Once novices had entered the Community, they still needed a preceptor, to instruct them in proper comportment and in the monastic rules and customs. In the first days of the Community, no preceptor was available for each novice, and as a result, according to the *Mahāvagga* (Vin I 44), some disciples behaved in reprehensible ways. People started to complain: "Look at these monks, sons of the Sākyans! They do not wear their robes correctly; they go through the village chatting and laughing; they talk in the refectory and make as much noise as brahmins at mealtime." The solution was to prescribe that each novice should be trained by a preceptor. There were two kinds of training: younger novices had to be taught the Doctrine and the Discipline; older ones had to be helped to make the transition from lay to monastic life, and their former attitudes had to be transformed into humility and obedience. This second kind of training was the hardest, since it is more difficult to teach older people (see above pp.3–4).

In the *Vinaya*, the relationship which develops between preceptor and pupil is compared to that of father and son. In truth, more than a comparison, the father-son relation was an institution in the Community: "the preceptor must look upon his pupil (*saddhivihārika*)[1] as a son; the pupil must look upon his preceptor as a father" (Vin I 45). Both the *Mahāvagga* (Vin I 46–49) and the *Cullavagga* (Vin II 222–227) dwell at length and in detail on the way a pupil was to behave toward his preceptor; in daily life, his duty was to act as a pupil, a servant and a son to his preceptor. For his part, the preceptor was responsible for his pupil. He had to see to his needs, for example, in providing him with robes. He also had to impart his knowledge to him, for example, in teaching him to eat as was the custom in the Community, or to walk in the street in a way befitting a monk. If the pupil became ill, his preceptor had to look after him. The pupil had to be submissive and obedient to his preceptor, whose permission was required, for example, if he wanted to give away his begging-bowl or his robes, and in many other aspects of his life: being of service to someone else, carrying messages, nursing someone or requesting treatment for himself, begging for someone else or accepting alms brought by a fellow-monk, going to the next village or to the cremation ground, or leaving his locality.

The preceptor had the right to dismiss his pupil for one of five reasons: if the pupil was not affectionate or polite enough towards him, if the pupil did not trust or respect him, or if he did not make progress under his guidance. However, the preceptor was prohibited from expelling his pupil from the monastic boundary (Vin I 84): if the pupil asked for his preceptor's forgiveness, the latter had to grant it and take him back as his pupil; otherwise he committed a serious offense (Vin I 54).

Other aspects of the relationship between preceptor and pupil are noteworthy. The pupil also had the right to give advice to his preceptor. If a preceptor lost heart with the practice of the religious life, or showed signs of weariness, his pupil was to encourage him and discuss the Doctrine with him, or find someone else more qualified to advise him. If a preceptor had come to misinterpret the Doctrine, his pupil was to try to correct him or to see to it that someone else corrected him. Thus the relationship between preceptor and pupil was not limited to preceptor's authority and pupil's obedience. It was a partnership for the purpose of inner progress, the preceptor's as much as the pupil's: "both must establish deference, respect and attachment to communal life between them, in order to grow prosperous and strong in this Doctrine and in this Discipline" (Vin I 45). In general, preceptors were not all Arahants. A preceptor could be learned about the Doctrine and the Discipline, and very virtuous, while still an "ordinary person" (*puthujjana*) in the matter of inner progress; in other words, he might still not be free from defilements. As a result, it was quite possible that he might feel dissatisfaction, discouragement or weariness, or that he might misinterpret the Doctrine or the Discipline. In this case, the duty of an intelligent pupil was to come to his preceptor's aid.[2]

It was necessary to fulfill certain conditions in order to become a preceptor. The *Mahāvagga* gives a long list of the required qualifications: a monk had to have received the Major Ordination at least ten years beforehand, and thereby to have acquired the title *Thera* (for such a nun, the title was *Therī*); moreover he had to be experienced and learned. Scandals sometimes occurred because of unintelligent preceptors being in charge of intelligent students; the situation was made worse if these pupils came from other religious sects. The incompetence of some preceptors led their pupils to leave the Community and go back to the religious sect they had formerly belonged to (Vin I 61, 69).

When the novice reached the age of twenty, and if his training had been successful, he was put forward by his preceptor as a candidate for the major Ordination, before a formal meeting of the Community (Vin I 94). Only after he had received the major Ordination did a pupil become a full member of the Community; but he still had to stay with his preceptor for another five years, which could be extended again if at the end he was not yet able fully to take part in preaching. In general, a monk became completely independent ten years after his major Ordination. Nevertheless, he still had to stay with his preceptor and look after him if he became ill.

The Authority of the Community: (1) the Various Categories of Rules

Novices had only ten rules to observe (Vin I 83–4).[3] In fact, these were not, properly speaking, rules or commandments, but precepts (*sikkhāpada*); their aim was to help train novices who, without being full members of the Community, had the right to share in its life as the pupils of full members. At the material level (food, clothes, and other necessities), there was not much difference between a full monk and a novice: in the eyes of lay followers, novices were monks just like their preceptors. But novices and female postulants (see p.135 note 3 above) were not allowed to take part in the formal meetings of the monastic Community or in its legal

Table 8.1. *Categories and numbers of rules for monks and nuns.*

	Number of Rules for monks/nuns
1. *Pārājika*–offenses entailing defeat	4 / 8
2. *Saṅghādisesa*–offenses which must be judged by a formal meeting of the Community	13 / 17
3. *Aniyata*–offenses whose classification is not determined (requiring evidence from a laywoman)	2 / 0
4. *Nissagiya Pācittiya*–offenses requiring confession and forfeiture of what has been improperly obtained	30 / 30
5. *Pācittiya*–offenses requiring confession	92 / 166
6. *Pāṭidesanīya*–lesser offenses requiring confession	4 / 8
7. *Sekhiyā*–precepts of good behavior	75 / 75
8. *Adhikaraṇa samatha*–procedural rules	7 / 7
Total:	227 / 311

acts until they had received the major Ordination; thereafter they had to obey the rules and precepts of the *Vinaya*. These rules, to be obeyed by monks and nuns, fall into eight different categories (see Table 8.1).

The most important of these rules concerned the offenses called *Pārājika,* for which there was no possibility of rehabilitation.

Offenses called *Saṅghādisesa* were also regarded as serious, but they only entailed punishment and permitted rehabilitation; they were to be judged and dealt with by the Community meeting formally for that purpose on three occasions: at the beginning of the judgment, at the start of the punishment, and at the end, to rehabilitate the culprit. Offenses in this category included touching a woman, accusing another monk without foundation, building a cell larger than prescribed in the regulations, and others.

Both rules called *Aniyata* were applicable only to monks; in order to judge the offense involved, the Community was to call a pious laywoman to witness. For example if a monk had remained alone behind closed doors in the company of a woman, his offense was not clear. If the monk had had sexual relations with her, he committed an offense entailing defeat; if he had only touched her, he committed an offense requiring judgment by a formal meeting of the Community; if he had only talked to her, his offense only entailed confession. Because of the difficulties of this kind of judgment, the Community required the testimony of a laywoman well-known for her devotion to the Three Jewels, in addition to the accused monk's statement, before it could reach a decision.

The rules called *Nissaggiya Pācittiya* concerned offenses which required confession and forfeiture of what had been improperly obtained or accepted; rules about money, discussed in Chapter 5, provide a good example of these.

The *Pācittiya* rules dealt with minor offenses requiring only confession: eating after noon, going to see a military parade, and so forth.

The *Pāṭidesanīya* rules were also concerned with offenses which had to be confessed and forgiven, notably on the issue of meals. According to the *Pāṭidesanīya* rule 4, for example, a monk living alone in the forest was not to eat food received from a stranger (Vin IV 182). If he did so, he had to confess his offense before a group of monks, or before a gathering of the Community: "Venerable ones, I have committed an offense which is blameworthy, improper, and needs to be declared publicly: I hereby confess it."

The *Vinaya* also contains seventy-five precepts concerning the good behavior of monks and nuns in everyday life; they are called *Sekhiyā dhammā*, and prescribe the correct ways to dress, eat, walk, and talk. Examples of what was dictated by the proper discipline were, "I put on my robe correctly. . ." (Vin II 185); "I walk in the village without laughing. . ." (Vin IV 187); "I do not make any noise with my mouth when I eat. . ." (Vin IV 197); "I do no lick my hands when I eat. . ." (Vin IV 198). The intention behind these precepts was to train individuals to be well-behaved, and to be models of good behavior for society.

The seven rules called *Adhikaraṇa samatha* concern legal procedures; their aim is to settle disputes in relation to each type of offense.

The *Mahā-Parinibbāna-sutta* (D II 154) recounts that the Buddha allowed his disciples to modify minor rules with the agreement of the Community; but according to the *Cullavagga* (cf. Vin II 288) the monks who took part in the first council in Rājagaha were not able to decide which of the rules constituted these "minor rules" referred to by the Buddha.

The Authority of the Community (ii): Punishment and Rehabilitation

The question of punishment is included in the disciplinary code of the *Vinaya*. First of all we must note that there was no corporal punishment in Buddhist monasticism. In particular, monks were forbidden to punish novices by depriving them of food (Vin I 84). In general, problems related to the discipline of novices did not come before the Community; they were resolved by their preceptors. The Community was directly involved, however, when the novice was put up for the major Ordination; then any member of the Community had a right to express his or her opposition. If their opposition turned out to be reasonable and well-founded, the Community refused to bestow the major Ordination. It was entitled to expel some novices judged to be unworthy, and let others stay as novices, without obtaining the major Ordination.

For monks and nuns who had received the major Ordination, the most serious offense entailed defeat (*Pāarājika*). How was this offense punished? One can say that it "entails permanent expulsion," but in fact neither expulsion nor any other punishment was possible after such an offense, because the offense itself excluded the culprit from membership of the Community. It may be compared to suicide: how is one to punish a suicide? Losing one's life is in itself sufficient punishment; it is also an automatic form of retribution. Monks who had committed offenses entailing defeat had committed suicide in relation to the Community.

On receiving the major Ordination, all new members were informed of these rules (Vin I 96–97), so that: (1) they were made clearly aware of the four most serious offenses (eight for nuns); (2) they were prepared to accept with full awareness that committing such an offense would deprive them of membership in the Community, and that this was automatic; (3) they were thus made responsible both for their membership in the Community and their possible exclusion from it, should that happen. Images and symbolic comparisons are given in the texts which explained to the new member the offenses and what they entailed. These are the examples from the first four *pārājikas*, applied to monks (Vin I 96–97):

1. *Sexual relations:* "as a beheaded man cannot live with the body alone, so a monk who has had sexual intercourse is not a monk anymore, he is not a disciple, a son of the Sākyans. From this offense you must try to abstain, for the rest of your life."
2. *Theft:* "as a dry leaf detached from the branch cannot become green again, so a monk who intentionally, takes what has not been given to him, be it a *pāda* [a small monetary unit], a *pāda*'s worth or more, is not a monk anymore. . ."
3. *Killing, encouraging someone to die or helping a suicide:* "as one cannot, with a stone broken in two, make a whole stone again, so a monk who knowingly kills a human being is not a monk anymore. . ."
4. *Boasting of superhuman perfections:* . . . As a palm tree with a broken top cannot grow again, so a monk who, for evil purpose and out of greed, untruthfully boasts of having attained any superhuman perfection, is not a monk anymore. . ."

These comparisons made very clear the nature of the offenses and their consequences. The punishment for them did not come from any outside authority, but automatically and simply from the culprit's conscience. Knowing that he had forfeited his membership in the Community, a "monk" who still took part in the Community's meetings and legal acts (*saṅgha kamma*) was being dishonest with himself; he was a "usurper." Legal procedures enacted by the Community could not in themselves bring about "expulsion." According to the code of jurisprudence of Buddhist monasticism, the Community was not entitled to judge monks or nuns in their absence, or to judge culprits who refused to acknowledge any serious offense of their own free will. What was involved here is only the individual's honesty and respect for the rules. Whether they were accused or not, whether an adverse judgment was passed against them or not, whether there was sufficient evidence or not, the "defeated" members had to leave the Community of their own volition. Whether they had been expelled or not, they were to know that they were no longer members of the Community. As a passage from the *Aṅguttara Nikāya* puts it: "Although he sits in the middle of the gathered Community, he is far away from the Community, and the Community is also far away from him" (A IV 201).

Although Buddhist monks and nuns were very strictly bound to obey these four (or eight) rules, there was no question of their taking solemn vows: they did not make any promises. They were only told that they had to attempt to avoid committing this kind of offense. The rules were not even commandments, but only advice given to the new member by the Community. Should a monk or nun fail in his or her attempt to avoid transgression, he or she was faced with two choices: either to abandon the monastic Community and go back to lay life before committing the offense, or to go back to lay life immediately after the offense, on confessing it.

Offenses in the other categories involved judgments, punishments, penances, confessions, rehabilitations. Let us start with the offenses called *Saṅghādisesa*, often glossed by scholars as "offenses entailing temporary expulsion." In fact, these offenses did not entail temporary expulsion so much as a "rehabilitation period" with four stages, depending on the type and seriousness of the offense: 1. It was decreed that the offender should undergo a probation period; 2. He or she was temporarily suspended at the beginning of the probation period; 3. He or she was placed under discipline; 4. He or she was rehabilitated. Any monk or nun was entitled to accuse another member of the Community of an offense in this category, but often the offender himself confessed the offense and asked to undergo a probation period. We have already noted that self-accusation was part of the declaration of purity made by monks before the reciting of the *Pātimokkha* during the ceremony of the *Uposatha*. The life of the Community rested on truthfulness and honesty, both toward others and toward oneself. If someone did not publicly acknowledge his offense, he was guilty of lying on purpose. The Buddha had this to say to Rāhula on the subject:

> If someone is not ashamed to tell a deliberate lie, his religious life is empty and wasted . . . and there is no evil of which he is incapable. So, Rāhula, you must train yourself in this way: "I will not lie, not even for fun."
>
> (M I 415)

There was no room for hypocrisy or secrecy. Anyone guilty of an offense had to acknowledge it openly and present himself of his own volition to receive punishment.

For most members of the Community there were three kinds of probation. (There is a fourth mentioned in the *Vinaya*, which was intended for those new candidates who came from other religious sects.) They were:

1. *Paṭicanna parivāsa:* this applied if someone had committed an offense from the *Saṅghādisesa* category and did not declare it. In this case, the length of probation depended on the number of days he or she had gone without confessing the offense.

2. *Suddhanta parivāsa:* this applied if someone, having committed several offenses of the *Saṅghādisesa* category,

could not remember when or exactly what they were. In this case the length of probation was calculated on the basis of the time elapsed since his or her major Ordination.

3. *Samodhāna parivāsa:* this applied if someone committed another offense of the *Saṅghādisesa* category during a period of probation. In this case, the period of probation was extended, and the extension calculated on the basis of the time elapsed between the beginning of the first probation period and the second offense.

These probations could not be imposed, annulled, extended or ended without a formal meeting of the Community. During the probation period, for example, a monk was subjected to a long list of prohibitions: he was not allowed to leave the monastery, to look for offenses committed by those members of the Community who imposed the probation period on him, to bestow Ordination or teach a novice, to preach to nuns (even if asked), to quarrel with fellow-monks, to give orders, to sit down in the presence of senior monks (*thera*) or to walk in front of them, or to approach lay followers. He had to be content with the last seat, the last bed, the last cell, the last dwelling in the Community. All the while, of course, he was not to commit the same offense again, or any other offense from the *Saṅghādisesa* category (Vin II 7–10, 31–72), Once the probation period was ended, a monk whose behavior had not improved might be required by the Community to undergo another probation period, followed by a period when he was "on parole." At the end of these two periods, if his behavior was still unsatisfactory, he had to remain under supervision of an experienced monk: this regulation is called *nissaya kamma*. During this period of dependence, the monk had still to obey the prohibitions outlined above.

The transgression of the *Nissaggiya Pācittiya* rules did not entail any punishment. The culprits had only to confess the offense and forfeit what was improperly obtained. If they had acquired an extra robe, for example, they had to confess the deed and give the robe to the Community. There was a special regulation concerning begging-bowls. We saw in

Chapter Four that *Nissaggiya Pācittiya* rule 21 allowed a monk to use an extra begging-bowl, provisionally, for ten days, and to ask for a new bowl or accept one if his own was too old (Vin III 242). Apart from these two exceptions, a monk who accepted or used a new begging-bowl had to give it back to the Community; it was then given to the first monk in order of seniority, and so on. (Seniority depended on the number of years spent as a member of the Community.) As a result, the culprit was taught a lesson in humility, since it was the bowl of the most junior member of the Community which came down to him with the following words: "Here is your begging-bowl, keep it until it is unusable" (Vin III 244–247).

The punishments inflicted for transgression of the *Pācittiya* rules were not very harsh. The literal sense of the term *pācittiya* contains the ideas of repentance, compensation and expiation; this is why I. B. Horner[4] refers to them as "rules of expiation," and French scholars as "offenses entailing penance" (*les fautes qui entraînent la pénitence*). However, the Pali *Vinaya* does not mention any penance or expiation for these offenses; on the contrary, confession is all they require. It is true that neither *pācittiya* nor its Sanskrit equivalent *prāyaścittika* have any etymological connection with the idea of confession; but we should keep in mind that some Sanskrit terms, or terms derived from the Sanskrit, are used in Pali Buddhist texts with a meaning different from that given by their etymology.

Since we are considering offenses entailing confession, let us take a closer look at the notion of confession in general in Buddhist monasticism. Before reciting the *Pātimokkha* during the ceremony of the *Uposatha*, monks and nuns declared and confessed their offenses: what was the nature and meaning of their confession? To whom did they confess, and who had the power to forgive them? In the *Vinaya*, offenses are referred to as *āpatti*, and the term can be used for all the categories of offense listed in the disciplinary code: *pārājikāpatti*, *saṅghādisesāpatti*, and so forth. Confession before the Community was called *āpatti desanā*, and the term *āpatti* can be translated "fault" or "offense"; it is sometimes translated as "sin," although the two concepts are, I believe, quite different. For example, in Buddhism, sexual intercourse is not considered a sin (*pāpa kamma*), but it constitutes a serious offense for a monk or nun, with respect to the Community's rules. Similarly, the *Pācittiya* rule 1 makes eating afer noon an offense, but that is not in itself a sin.

So there exists in Buddhism a difference between a "sin" and an offense; the Buddhist equivalent of the notion of sin seems to be *pāpa kamma*, "demeritorious action," which is to be clearly distinguished from the concept of an offense against a conventional set of rules. In Buddhism, *pāpa kamma*, "demeritorious action," as well as "*puñña kamma*," meritorious action, both come under the jurisdiction of the universal law called *kamma niyāma*, "the law of act and result" (cf.Paṭis II 78, As 272), and so Buddhist texts refer to demeritorious actions as *loka vajjā*, "universal offenses." On the other hand, the term *āpatti* denotes the transgression by monks of codified institutional rules; they are called *sammuti vajjā*, "conventional offense," and are not necessarily all included in the class of universal offenses.[5] For example, the conventional *Pācittiya* rules 53 (for monks) and 134 (nuns) forbid swimming, but swimming as such does not constitute a demeritorious act in Buddhism. On the other hand, killing an animal is a demeritorious act, not because it is the first Buddhist precept, but because of the universal law, according to which anyone who kills an animal is bound to have feelings of hatred. Since deeds performed under the influence of hatred are demeritorious, killing an animal is a "sin," whether it is the action of lay people or monks, Buddhist or non-Buddhist; everyone suffers the same automatic retribution (*kamma vipāka*) for it. Thus a monk who kills an animal performs a demeritorious act, and in addition transgresses the *Pācittiya* rule 61 (Vin IV 124) (nuns' *Pācittiya* 142). The Community could only concern itself with the conventional aspect of such an offense, since it had no authority to implement the universal law: there does not exist any institution possessed of such authority. These rules required the culprit to confess his or her offense before the Community, before a fellow monk or nun or before a group of them; promising through their confession to take better care of living creatures in the future, they were exonerated from the institutional offense of killing an animal, but not from the universal offense, for which they would still suffer retribution in accordance with the law of *kamma*. Confession inside the Buddhist Community was simply a piece of institutional regulation with no universal validity. At the social level, it emphasized the fact that members of the Community did not have a private life. At the psychological level, confession, besides encouraging monks to beware of future temptations, helped unburden their mind, and this was a basic necessity on the path of inner progress.

Other Sanctions

Other punishments were imposed by the Community depending on the type of offense. The legal act of the Community called *tajjanīya kamma,* for example, concerned those who quarrelled, tried to provoke a schism (*Saṅghādisesa* rules 10 and 11; nuns' *Saṅghādisesa* 14 and 15), or had improper relationships with lay people (*Saṅghādisesa* rule 13; nuns' *Saṅghādisesa* 17). They were first heard by the Community, then accused of the relevant offense. If the Community found them to be guilty, they were punished accordingly: they were deprived of certain privileges and subjected to a number of restrictions until a formal meeting of the Community lifted the punishment.

Another legal act of the Community, called *pabbājanīya kamma,* entailed expelling monks or nuns from their dwelling. The Community imposed this form of punishment on a group of monks from the monastery in Kīṭāgiri who had behaved improperly, dancing and singing with women, using perfumes and garlands. The two Elders, Sāriputta and Moggallana were sent to Kīṭāgiri to expel them (Vin II 8–14; cf. M I 473–481). A later historical chronincle, the *Mahāvaṃsa*

(Mv XXXIII 95), recounts that the same punishment was inflicted to a monk from the Mahāvihāra who had personally accepted a monastery given to him by king Vattagāmaṇī-Abhaya (29–17 B.C.) as a token of friendship.

The legal act called *ukkhepanīya kamma* punished someone for one of the three following reasons: if they remained without confessing an offense, without making amends, or without renouncing a wrong belief. The punishment included a number of prohibitions, similar to the ones imposed on monks and nuns during their probation period. The punishment was lifted when the culprit acknowledged his or her offense and asked for forgiveness.

A monk who harbored false opinions about the Doctrine or the Discipline was to be warned on three successive occasions by his fellow-monks (*Pācittiya* 68; nuns' *Pācittiya* 146); if he still clung to his false opinion, he committed an offense. A monk who associated with him also committed an offense (*Pācittiya 69; nuns'* Pācittiya 147). A novice who upheld false opinions was also to be given advice on three successive occasions (*Pācittiya* 70); if he refused the advice, he was told: "Novice, hereafter you should not indicate the Blessed One as your teacher. You cannot live even two or three days with monks. Please go wherever you wish." If a monk gave shelter or protection to such a guilty novice, he also committed an offense in the same category (Vin IV 134–140; nuns' *Pācittiya* 148).

Another kind of punishment was called *paṭisāraṇiya kamma*, the act of reconciliation; it was inflicted on monks and nuns who had annoyed a devoted layman or laywoman, quarrelled with a lay follower or in any way undermined his or her faith. It required the offender to go before the lay person and ask for forgiveness. If he or she was ashamed to go alone, the Community had to appoint someone to accompany them. The culprit was then to approach the lay follower and say: "Forgive me, householder; I am at peace with you." If the lay follower granted forgiveness all was well; otherwise, the appointed companion was to speak for him; if the lay follower still did not grant forgiveness, the offending monk had to confess the offense to his or her companion in the lay follower's presence (Vin II 15–18).

The punishment called *brahmadaṇḍa* was called "the harshest punishment." It was inflicted on arrogant monks or nuns: no member of the Community was to talk to or advise the culprit. The Community imposed it on the monk Channa, former charioteer of prince Gotama, because of his arrogance towards the Community (Vin II 290–292).

Disputes arising on matters of Doctrine or of Discipline were to be resolved by the Community. In the case of a quarrel, the Community was entitled to organize a referendum (Vin II 96), either by an open vote or by a secret ballot, and could settle the dispute in accordance with the opinion expressed by the majority (as long as it reflected the truth).

All judgments pronounced by the Community shared various characteristics. In all cases, with the two exceptions of the *brahmadaṇḍa* inflicted on the monk Channa and the *pakāsanīya kamma* inflicted on Devadatta,[6] the offender had to be present at a formal meeting of the Community and accused of a specific offense. What authority imposed the punishment? What were the limits of the Community's freedom to take decisions? What were the criteria for judgment? According to Buddhist jurisprudence, competent authority rested with the Doctrine and the Discipline: decisions by the Community were always to be in agreement with the Doctrine as it was preached by the Buddha (*dhammo desito*) and with the Discipline as it was established by the Buddha (*vinayo paññatto*).

The Authority of the Doctrine and of the Discipline

Numerous passages from the *Vinaya* show that the Buddha wished his Community to be an independent institution, without a leader. The *Mahā-Parinibbāna-sutta* (D II 62; cf. S V 152), for example, recounts how the Buddha told the venerable Ānanda Thera that he did not intend to control the Community or to have it depend on him.

A few months after the Buddha's death, the venerable Ānanda and the highest dignitary in the Magadha country, the brahmin Vassakāra, had a discussion; Vassakāra asked Ananda if the Buddha had appointed a monk to be leader of the Community after his death, and its "refuge." Ānanda answered in the negative. Vassakāra then asked if the Community had appointed a monk to such a position. Again Ananda answered in the negative. Then Vassakāra asked again: "Venerable Ananda, if there is no leader or refuge, on what basis can the Community be unified?" Ānanda answered: "Brahmin, we are not without refuge; we do have a refuge. We take refuge in the Doctrine." The dignitary did not understand the distinctive character of the Community's organization, so Ānanda had to explain: "A Code of Rules has been established for the members of the Community; all the members of a local Community gather together on the day of the *Uposatha* in order to recite it. If a member has committed a transgression, it is announced during this meeting; the other monks present deal with the matter according to justice. No one is forced or coerced into it. The Doctrine and the Discipline alone govern us." Vassakāra then asked another question: "Venerable Ānanda, is there a monk whom you respect, revere and on whom you rely?" This time Ānanda gave an affirmative answer, which confused the dignitary: "When I asked you whether there was a monk appointed by the Community to be your leader or your refuge, you answered "no." Now when I ask you if there is a monk whom you respect, revere and on whom you rely, you answer "yes"! How am I supposed to understand this?" Ānanda explained that the Buddha had praised the ten virtues of trustworthy monks,[7] and that if monks found in their midst someone possessed of these ten virtues, they would respect him, revere him and listen to him. Vassakāra was satisfied with this answer. Ānanda's explanations characterize the constitution and organization of the Community in the following ways: 1. It had no leader, no "king";[8] 2. It was always ready to pay homage and listen to a monk who was virtuous, wise and advanced on the path of inner progress; 3. There was no centralized authority and power.

The Community preserved its unity and discipline, although its members lived in groups in different areas. In certain cases, a group of four monks was entitled to represent the Community, but twenty members at least had to be gathered in order to pass a sentence or implement a disciplinary procedure independently from other groups. These groups had no separate identity; whatever their origin, they lived under the same constitution and according to rules valid for all members of the Community. Disagreements and problems were resolved locally by each group in accordance with the code of discipline, in meetings chaired by the most senior and wise monk present. When two or more groups of monks gathered together, they automatically formed one single group and organized their meeting under the chairmanship of one monk specially appointed for the occasion.

Endnotes

1. *Saddhivihārika:* literally "one who lives under the same roof as, one who shares accomodation with"; thus the term implies that novices lived with their teachers.
2. If a preceptor abandoned the religious life or left to join another religious sect, the Community appointed another such "teacher" (*ācariya*) to take over his pupil, who had the same relationship with him as the one he had had with his former preceptor.
3. [See Appendix 3.]
4. See *Book of the discipline*, vol.2, p.3 note 4.
5. Nonetheless, all universal offenses are also included in one way or another in the Community's code of discipline, as conventional offenses.
6. This punishment was inflicted on Devadatta in his absence, because of his attempt to provoke a schism in the Community. It represented an exceptional sanction, only ever imposed on Devadatta, and only mentioned once in the *Vinaya*. Through this legal act, the Community empowered the venerable Sāriputta Thera to denounce Devadatta's attitude before the people of Rājagaha (Vin II 189).

7. These ten virtues are: he must (1) be virtuous (2) be learned about the Doctrine and the Discipline (3) be contented (4) be experienced in the first four stages of meditation (*jhāna*) (5) have miraculous powers (6) be capable of hearing words spoken at a distance (7) be capable of reading other people's minds (8) be capable of knowing his previous lives (9) be capable of perceiving where a dead person has been reborn (10) be free from all defilements.
8. Centuries later, however, the Community appointed itself leaders. Nowadays, the monks' leader in Thailand is called *Sangharāja* (Thai *Somdet Phrasangkharaat,* king of the Community"), whose position is recognized by the state. In Sri Lanka, there are "Great Leaders" (*Mahā Nāyaka*) appointed by various congregations of monks; but even today these leaders are not personally entitled to expel or punish a monk, or to take any legal decision. They simply chair meetings. They are always elected through a secret ballot. In Thailand, the *Sangharāja* is officially appointed by the king, but with the monks'approval.

Conclusion

This study of the discipline and organization of the monastic Community illustrates the fundamentally ethical dimension of Buddhist monasticism. The codification of rules and precepts helped to promote a favorable environment for the religious life; the rules were necessary both to insure the continued existence of the Community and to secure and protect the rights and duties of its individual members.

Nonetheless, for Buddhism, even the most virtuous monk or nun could not reach the ultimate goal simply by being virtuous. Ethical conduct was essential, but as a means to the end of inner progress: this was why the ethical dimension was necessary to the monastic life. Ethical conduct (*sīla*) was the foundation of mental discipline (*samādhi*), mental discipline the foundation of the highest wisdom (*pañña*), and wisdom led the individual to be free from all defilements and to comprehend ultimate Reality: to obtain Release (*vimutti*). The Buddha told his disciples:

> Monks, the aim of the religious life is not to gain material profit, nor to win veneration, nor to reach the highest morality, nor to be capable of the highest mental concentration. Monks, the ultimate end of the religious life is the unshakeable liberation of the mind. This is the essence. This is the goal.
> (M I 192–197)

This Release allowed the disciple to live "for the benefit of the many, for the happiness of the many, out of compassion for the world" (Vin II 22). The Arahant both tasted the happiness of freedom and lived a life of religious service to others.

Appendix 1

Nuns

Women who leave home for homelessness in the Doctrine and Discipline taught by the Tathāgata *are capable of reaching the (four) stages on the Path of Liberation.*[1]

(Vin II 254)

Women play a significant part in the *Sutta-piṭaka* and in the *Vinaya-piṭaka*. There were many women among the Buddha's benefactors who faithfully supported the new "religion." Lay women such as Visākhā Migāra-Mātā, Sujātā, Bandulā, Mallikā, Khujuttarā, and others, showed great interest in the Buddha's teachings and reached the higher stages of inner progress. Some housewives such as Veḷukaṇṭhakī Nanda-Mātā attained the state of Non-returner (*anāgāmi*) (A I 88, II 164, IV 63–4).

Naturally, some women wished to join the Buddhist Community as nuns. During the Buddha's first visit to Kapilavatthu, his aunt and foster-mother, Mahā Pajāpatī Gotamī, asked that an Order of nuns be established; but the Buddha did not grant her request. She asked and was refused twice more. Some time later, Mahā Pajāpatī Gotamī, Rāhula-Mātā (Gotama's former wife), and some other Sākyan women traveled a long way on foot to Vesāli to show their determination and ask the Buddha to establish an Order of nuns. Finally, through the intercession of the Venerable Ānanda, who himself asked three times and was refused, the Buddha granted their request (Vin II 253–56).

Why did the Buddha decline at first? He might have

thought that the time had not yet come to establish an Order of nuns. We can offer another hypothesis: all the women who first came to him were relatives of his from the Sākyan family. If the Buddha had acceded to their request at once, some of his opponents might have thought it scandalous; his hesitation spared him such criticism. It should be noted that, although the request to establish the Order of nuns originated wholly with Sākyan women, many brahmin women joined the Order after it was established.

The Buddha's initial hesitation also shows that he anticipated a number of problems which might arise for nuns, especially in the course of their everyday life: an Order of nuns might be vulnerable, and need the protection of future generations. And indeed, as he had foreseen, there were unfortunate incidents. For example, a young nun was raped in the Andhavana forest; because of this, nuns were forbidden to travel or dwell in forests (Vin III 35, Dh-a II 49). On another occasion, while nuns were away, their huts were burned down (Vin IV 303). Another story tells of a group of nuns traveling to Sāvatthi; towards night time, they found a house and asked to spend the night. The brahmin housewife told them: "Wait until the head of the household comes back and gives you permission." When the brahmin arrived in the night and saw the nuns, he immediately threw them out with the words: "Out with these shaven-headed whores!" (Vin IV 273–275).

The new Community had to conform to the norms customary in the society of that time, as is shown by the "Eight Important Conditions" imposed by the Buddha when he allowed the Order to be established. These eight rules (Vin II 255, IV 52, A 4 276–277), which were to be "observed, respected, honored and revered by a nun, and never transgressed for as long as she lived," were:

1. A nun, even if ordained for a hundred years, must greet a monk with deference, even if he has been ordained that very day; she must rise up from her seat, salute him with joined hands, and show him proper respect.

2. A nun is forbidden to spend the Rainy Season Retreat in a district where there is no monk.

3. Every fortnight, a nun is to ask two things of the monks: the date of the Uposatha ceremony,[2] and to preach the Doctrine.

4. At the end of the Rainy Season Retreat, a nun must address "the triple invitation" to both the Order of monks and the Order of nuns: she must ask whether anyone has seen, heard or suspected anything (against her).

5. A nun who has committed a serious offense must undergo the *mānatta* discipline [a kind of temporary probation] before both Orders.

6. Ordination as a nun is to be sought from both Orders only after a postulant has followed the six precepts for two years.[3]

7. A nun is on no account to revile or abuse a monk.

8. (From the very first day of the Nuns' Order) monks can give admonition and advice to nuns, but nuns cannot do so to monks.

It seems that in recounting how the Order of nuns came to be established, the early disciples who redacted the texts wanted to show that it was a deliberate and careful decision on the part of the Buddha. The most remarkable aspect of the story is the answer the Buddha gave to the Venerable Ānanda, when asked whether womanhood was an obstacle in reaching any of the four stages on the path of Liberation. The Buddha replied clearly that womanhood was not at all an obstacle; on the contrary, women were quite capable of reaching the four stages of liberation, just like men (Vin II 254). This answer alone shows that the Buddha's refusal was motivated by social and practical considerations. Years later, when asked by a wandering mendicant whether there were in Rājagaha any nuns who had reached the perfect state, the Buddha emphatically answered: "not merely a hundred, nor two, nor three, four or five hundred, but far more are those nuns, my disciples, who by the elimination of defilements have here and now realized by direct knowledge the freedom of mind and wisdom that is without defilements, and who abide (in that realization)" (M I 490).

The canonical text entitled *Therīgāthā* (Verses of Elder Nuns) is an anthology of seventy-three poems (522 verses) – exclamations of religious joy – attributed to seventy-two nuns who have reached the higher stages of inner progress. It is noteworthy that several of these poems present the nuns as possessing "the three knowledges" (*tevijjā*).[4] In canonical texts, to possess "the three knowledges" means to be an Arahant (e.g. M I 21–23, 183–4, 278–9, 347–8, II 20–21, 226–7). In describing nuns as possessing "the three knowledges," the *Therīgāthā* is probably giving an indirect response to Brahmanism, where women were not allowed to attain "the three knowledges" (*trayī vidyā*), which meant knowledge of the three *Vedas*. The Buddha had explicitly opposed his interpretation of the familiar term "the three knowledges" to the brahmanical one: "Brahmins interpret 'the three knowledges' in their own way, but in the Discipline of the Noble Ones,' 'the three knowledges' have a different meaning" (M II 144, A I 163–6). Thus in attributing "the three knowledges" to nuns, the compilers of the canonical texts might well have meant to say: "Look, Buddhist women are indeed capable of attaining the true 'three knowledges'."

So the Buddhist Order of nuns, which was established in the sixth century B.C., looks rather modern: women were able to work towards their own liberation by renouncing domesticity and family life. The birth of an organised community of renunciate women in a society where a woman lived her whole life in a state of submission – in childhood to her parents, in marriage to her husband, and in widowhood to her sons – was one of the most important events in the history of religions.

The organization of the Order of nuns was parallel to that of the monks: like the monks, they possessed a complete Code of Discipline (*Pātimokkha*), their legal acts (*vinaya-kamma, saṅgha-kamma*) were the same, and they also had two Ordinations, the Minor (*pabbajjā*) and the Major (*upasampadā*). Ten years after her Major Ordination, a nun was also called an "Elder" (*Therī*). Nuns organized their communal life independently, according to their own Code of Discipline, but with help and advice from monks. Monks had the right to advise nuns, not to control them.

The *Aṅguttara Nikāya* gives a long list of outstanding nuns: Khemā Therī, for example, was foremost among those who possessed great wisdom, Uppalavaṇṇā Therī among those who had super-human powers, Paṭācārā Therī among the experts in the Code of Discipline, Dhammadinnā Therī among preachers of the Doctrine, and Nandā Therī among those skilled in meditation (A I 25). As we saw earlier (pp.133–4) several discourses from the *Sutta-piṭaka* show that nuns took part in preaching (e.g. M I 299–305, S IV 374, A V 53–58).

Historical chronicles and archaelogical evidence indicate that the Order of nuns existed until at least the tenth century A.D. in Sri Lanka, when it seems to have disappeared because of social and political problems. In particular, when the country passed through periods of war and foreign invasion, the Order of nuns could not function successfully. There is some evidence that nuns may have existed in Burma for a little longer. Nowadays in Theravāda Buddhist countries some women wear yellow or white robes and observe eight or ten Precepts, but without being ordained. According to the *Vinaya*, the Order of monks cannot confer either the Minor or the Major Ordinations on women. This can be done only by nuns in the presence of both Orders. Moreover, such an ordination should take place in the presence of a minimum of five Elder nuns. That quorum is no longer available, which means that the Order of nuns has disappeared, and such a legal act (*saṅgha-kamma*) is no longer possible.

Endnotes

1. See Glossary under *sotāpanna*, etc.
2. [See pp.123–4 above.]
3. See pp.135–6 and note 3 above.

4. These are (1) the memory of former lives, (2) knowledge of the death and rebirth of others, and (3) knowledge of the destruction of one's mental defilements (e.g. A I 163–166). In other canonical texts (e.g. S I 146, A I 105, Iti 98, Vin II 87), the "three knowledges" refer to the capacity (1) to perform miracles, (2) to read the minds of others, and to (3) the knowledge of the destruction of one's mental defilements.

Appendix 2

Lay people

I praise neither monks nor laypeople who behave badly. If they behave badly, neither lay people nor monks can lead right, just and virtuous lives.
I praise both monks and laypeople who behave properly. If laypeople and monks behave properly, they can both lead right, just and virtuous lives. . .

(M II 197; S.V 19; A I 69)

Many scholars view Theravāda Buddhism as an essentially monastic religion. There is some truth in this, but the matter is often misunderstood because the position of lay people in Buddhism has not been sufficiently studied.

The *Vinaya* texts show that the Buddha converted lay people to his new religious movement from the very beginning. The first people to accept him as their religious master were two merchants called Tapassu and Bhallika (Vin I 3, A I 25), who met the Buddha by chance on a business trip. This happened soon after the Enlightenment, a few weeks before the first discourse and the establishment of Buddhist monasticism. A few months later, the young monk Yasa's father and mother in turn accepted the Buddha as their religious master (Vin I 15–20). For these lay people, whose former religious allegiance we do not know, converting to Buddhism did not entail renouncing life in the world: they simply became the followers of the Buddha and his teaching.

Many people adopted Buddhism as their religion on the occasion of the Buddha's first visit to the town of Rājagaha, only a few months after his Enlightenment (Vin I 35–37).

During the next forty-five years, the Buddha met a multitude of people and converted very many of them. In order to join him, many of these people probably gave up their traditional religion, Brahmanism. Rich brahmins, such as Jānussoni (D I 235, M I 175) and Pokkarasāti (D I 87) renounced their religion to become the Buddha's followers. Other lay people came to Buddhism from Jainism. When one of them, a householder from Nālanda called Upāli, came home after his conversion, he gave instructions to his servants: "From now on, the doors of my house are open for the Buddha and the members of his Community; they are closed for Jain monks" (M I 380); but the Buddha advised Upāli to continue his material support of his former religious master, Nigaṇṭha Nātaputta. The Sākyan called Vappa (A II 196) and general Sīha from Vesāli (A IV 179, Vin I 233) also renounced Jainism to become Buddhists.

According to stories recounted in the *Nikāya* texts, two great kings, contemporaries of the Buddha, Seniya Bimbisāra from the Magadha country, and Pasenadi from the Kosala country, became followers of Buddhism. King Bimbisāra was converted a few months after the Enlightenment (Vin I 35), and king Pasenadi probably one or two years later. When he first met the Buddha, king Pasenadi complained that the Buddha was still too young, and could not possibly be the Enlightened One; to this the Buddha replied that there were four things which should not to be despised or disregarded simply because of their youth: a noble prince, a snake, fire and a monk. This dialogue between the king and the Buddha is called the *Dahara-sutta* (S I 68); it occurs in a section of the *Saṃyutta-nikāya*, called *Kosala Saṃyutta*, which is entirely devoted to the religious dialogues of king Pasenadi with the Buddha. Several discourses addressed by the Buddha to king Bimbisāra are also mentioned in the *Nikāya* texts.

Lay people who adopted Buddhism as their religion, whether brahmins or kings, noblemen or peasants, paid allegiance to the Master (*Buddha*), to his Teaching (*Dhamma*) and to his religious Community (*Saṅgha*); these made up a Buddhist "trinity" called "the Threefold Refuge" (*tisaraṇa*) or "the Threefold Jewel" (*ratanattaya*). When lay people wished to become Buddhist, they would declare: "I take refuge in the Buddha; I take refuge in the Teaching; I take refuge in the Community."[1] Lay followers were called "devotees" (male or female, *upāsaka, upāsikā*); by this formula of "taking refuge" (*saraṇāgamana*), they announced their admiration and support for the Buddha, his Teaching and his religious Community (A III 206, IV 220, S V 395). There was no baptism ceremony or any other such ritual to mark their conversion to the new religion.

In everyday life, lay Buddhists have to observe the Five Precepts (*Pañca-Sīla*),[2] which are:

1. To abstain from destroying life;
2. To abstain from stealing;
3. To abstain from illicit sexual relations;
4. To abstain from telling lies;
5. To abstain from liquor that causes intoxication and heedlessness.

Some of the items in this list can in some respects be compared to the ten Commandments of Judeo-Christianity; but the Five Precepts do not claim a divine origin. Moreover, they are not commandments, but principles of education (*sikkhāpadāni*), which lay followers freely accept to follow, when they make the following declarations: "I accept to observe the precept to abstain from destroying life; I accept to observe the precept to abstain from stealing," and so on.

The first of these five precepts represented a noteworthy departure from the religion which was dominant at the time of the Buddha. The attitude of non-violence, loving-kindness and compassion which it advocates conflicted with that of orthodox Brahmanism, which attributed great importance to animal sacrifice. The Buddha repeated this precept in various discourses (A I 146, II 203, IV 220, S II 68–80, IV 109), and explicitly advised king Pasenadi to abstain from performing violent sacrifices (S I 75).

At first sight the Five Precepts appear to be purely negative; but they also have a positive aspect, as will be shown in the following examples:

1. *To abstain from destroying life:* this precept does not simply prohibit killing; it also advocates the protection and care of living beings. In following this precept, lay followers uphold the right to live of all living beings.
2. *To abstain from stealing:* here lay followers not only pledge not to steal or take what does not belong to them, but also agree to protect what belongs to others; they recognize their neighbors' right to private property.
3. *To abstain from illicit sexual relations:* it is through this precept that Buddhism specifically condemns adultery, whether it involves husband or wife; here lay people also recognize the legitimacy of marriage, as well the necessity of faithfulness between husband and wife and the unsuitability of damaging, directly or indirectly, that faithfulness.
4. *To abstain from telling lies:* lay followers undertake to avoid lying and more positively to speak only the truth and to be honest with others.
5. *To abstain from liquor that causes intoxication and heedlessness:* this precept is directly related to the doctrine of Mindfulness, to which Buddhism attaches great value. According to it, many offenses might be committed in a state of inattention induced by intoxicants such as alcohol: these can disturb the mind's capacity for concentration. More positively, the precept exhorts lay followers to remain mindful in word and deed.

Considered in their positive aspects, the Five Precepts embodied important social values: the canonical texts regard their observance as the basis of stability, harmony and lack of crime in society (D II 58–77). Lay followers who abided by the Five Precepts are compared to jewels and to lotus flowers (A III 206).

Advice on How to Lead a Happy Lay Life

Not everyone in the world would or could become a monk or a nun. The Buddha realized a few weeks after his Enlightenment that most people want to enjoy sensual pleasures (cf. Vin I 4–5). So the "new religion" had to give them advice on how to lead just and contented family lives. Lay people on their side were ready to receive such advice; one day, for example, a householder called Dighajānu visited the Buddha and asked him: "Blessed one, we are ordinary lay people, and we lead the life of householders, with wife and children. Can the Blessed One teach us how to find happiness in this and in future lives? (A IV 281)"

In the canon, a number of discourses addressed to lay people insist on social justice and harmony. The *Sigālovāda-sutta* (D III 180) gives advice on how to preserve friendliness and harmony between members of society. The *Parābhava-sutta* (Sn 91–115) explains how someone might become poor and unhappy, and how to avoid doing so. The *Vasala-sutta* (Sn 116–142) shows how to become respectable and of good standing through proper behavior. Buddhism was absolute and unequivocal in its disregard for the privileges or disadvantages related to birth, profession or social status such as caste. It resolutely ignored all arbitrary prohibitions and regulations, whether ritual or social.[3]

There is even room for financial advice in these discourses: how to earn, spend and save money (*Vyaggapajja-sutta*, A IV 281; *Sigālovāda-sutta*, D III 180), and how economically disadvantageous it is to indulge in vices such as alcoholism or betting games (A III 252, D III 236, Ud p.86–87). Many discourses on financial success were delivered to Anāthapiṇḍika (A I 261, II 45–48, 64–66, III 204, 206). People were not forbidden to become rich, provided they employed honest means. Lay people were advised to abstain from five kinds of commerce: slaves, weapons, meat, alcohol and poisons (A III 208). A number of discourses take the view that wealth can positively contribute to the success of lay life. The *Cakkavatti-Sīhanāda-sutta* argues that poverty, on the other hand, generates immorality and crimes such as theft and murder (D III 67). Therefore, according to this discourse, the first duty of a king is to be generous and charitable. He must not be greedy and attached to wealth and property; rather, he must use them for the benefit and happiness of his people.

Regarding family life, the *Sigālovāda-sutta* teaches ways of preserving friendship and harmony between husband and wife, and between parents and children (D III 180). A man's duties towards his parents, his wife and his children are specified in the *Mahā-Maṅgala sutta* (Sn 257–268); and another discourse addressed to Anāthapiṇḍika's daughter-in-law describes how a wife must behave toward her husband (A IV 91). The *Nakula-sutta* gives a list of eight essential qualities which the ideal wife must possess (A III 295). The *Sigālovāda-sutta* insists that husbands should never be unfaithful; they must respect and trust their wife and avoid making her unhappy. One day the elderly householder Nakula Pitā told the Buddha:

> Blessed one, when my wife was brought to my house, she was a mere girl, and I was only a boy. I cannot recall having been unfaithful to her, not even in thought. Blessed one, we both want to live together in this way, in this life and in our future lives.
>
> (A II 61)

His wife Nakula Mātā expressed the same feelings about her husband. One day the Buddha visited them when they were both sick, and Nakula Pitā spoke of his wife. The Buddha said to him: "You are lucky, householder, to have a wife like Nakula Mātā, who is full of compassion, who desires your happiness and who gives you good advice" (A III 298). Although this story celebrates the value of married love, the monks found room for it in their canon: they probably thought that it would provide a good model of marital harmony and happiness for lay people. The Buddha compared the good householder, who does his best to secure a just and happy life for his wife and children, to the great blossoming *sāla* tree (*Shorea robusta:* A I 151, III 43). It is important to note here that at the time of the Buddha, people in different social groups had various customs regarding marriage; Buddhism chose monogamy for its lay followers (cf. S I 37, Sn 290, Jā VI 286–287), and provided arguments in its favor. The *Aṅguttura-nikaya* (II 57–58) develops the following comparison:

marriage between a virtuous man and a virtuous woman can be compared to the marriage of a god and a goddess. On the other hand, marriage between a virtuous man and an immoral woman is like that of a god with a corpse, between an immoral man and a virtuous woman like that of a corpse with a goddess, and between two immoral spouses like that of two corpses.

Lay Life and Renunciation

In the eyes of society at that time, one became truly a "layman" by becoming a householder: that is, by getting married and setting up a home. But the point of marriage was to have children. With the arrival of a family, a layman needed a certain level of affluence in order to support wife and children and make them happy. Once committed to this kind of life, he would not in general want to renounce his home; on the contrary, he would tend to remain strongly attached to it.

However, Buddhism did not want its lay followers to be immoderate in their enjoyment of sensual pleasures, and to forget completely the value of renunciation; lay people were advised to avoid an excess of luxury. To obey the Five Precepts, lay Buddhists had to renounce a number of vices and the pleasures they afford, such as illicit sexual relations (Third Precept), hunting animals (First Precept), and so forth. They were encouraged to take advantage of the opportunities which were offered to them to practice renunciation in a limited way. On the days of the full and of the new moon, for example, they were to obey the Eight Precepts (*Uposatha-sīla*) instead of the Five.[4] (When taken in this way as part of Eight Precepts, the third prescribed complete abstinence from sex, and not merely abstinence from illicit sexual relations.) Taking the Eight Precepts constituted a provisional and partial form of renunciation (cf. A I 205–207, IV 248, 258, Sn 400, 401). Some particularly devout lay followers observed ten Precepts[4] permanently while continuing to live at home: a layperson taking the ten Precepts renounced, like monks and nuns, all sexual relations and all dealings with money. The *Nikaya* texts call those who took the Ten Precepts "lay householders dressed in white and leading a life of chastity at home" (D I 211, III 117, 124, 210; M I 491, III 261; A I 74, III 295). They are contrasted with those "lay householders dressed in white and enjoying sensual pleasures at home". Like the Christian virgins and widows in the first centuries who remained at home and abstained from all sexual relations, these Buddhist laymen put into practice monastic principles of renunciation while living at home. We are not told why they did not enter the monkhood. They may have been unable to renounce family life completely for all kinds of reasons, such as having to take care of elderly parents, or other pressing difficulties.

Some lay followers went further and gave up family life altogether in order better to follow the precepts. A householder named Ugga from Hattigāmaka gave away his wife and his three maidservants to a respectable man, after he had formally obtained their consent (A IV 214). Strangely enough, however, once he found himself alone, he did not enter the monastic Community, but remained at home to continue with his religious practice. Perhaps he wanted to live alone at home, on a minimum income and with minimum spendings, free from family worries; or perhaps he wanted to travel far and wide between towns and villages, spreading the Doctrine as a lay preacher, since he was not an ordinary Buddhist, but a scholar well versed in the Buddha's teachings (A I 26, S IV 109). One day someone asked Ugga what he did when a monk came to visit him. He answered simply: "I ask him to preach the Doctrine. If he preaches, I listen to him. If he does not preach, I preach to him" (A IV 211).

Other householders, such as Citta, from the town of Maccikāsaṇḍa where he held the office of treasurer (Vin II 15), and Upāli from Nālanda (M I 371) are also described as lay people with substantial knowledge of the Buddha's Teaching. Citta's knowledge of the Doctrine was not limited to theory; it included practice as well (S IV 298). The *Nikāya* texts regard him as the ideal lay disciple (A I 88, II 164, III 451). His conversations with monks are recorded in the *Citta-samyutta* (S IV 282 ff); he sometimes held debates with Jain monks and tried to convert them.

Many lay followers, both men and women, reached the highest stages of inner progress: such as that of *Sotāpanna*, "entering the current" (the first stage towards *nibbāna*), *Sakadāgāmi*, "once-returner" (the second stage: one who will be reborn as a human being only once more), and *Anāgāmi*, "non-returner" (the third stage: no further human rebirth) (A III 347, M I 490). Anāthapiṇḍika reached the stage of *Sotāpanna*, as did Visākhā while still a young girl; she later reached the state of *Sakadāgāmi* (Dhp-a I 406ff.). The householder Citta reached the state of *Anāgāmi* and attained the fourth meditative state (S IV 298). The *Majjhima-nikāya* (I 290) tells us that "the number of lay people, both men and women, who reached the highest stages of inner progress, was not only one, two, or one hundred or five hundred, but much more than that, at Rājagaha."

Some of them – although only a small number according to the canonical texts – reached the state of Arahant. Suddhodana, the Buddha's elderly father, reached it while listening to a discourse preached by his son. Yasa, the wealthy young man (Vin I 15–20), and Khemā, king Bimbisāra's wife (Thī–a 126), reached it before entering the monastic life. The question is: what was to become of such a lay Arahant? Should he or she continue to live at home? Postcanonical texts say that lay people who became Arahants were faced with a decision: either they joined the monastic Community, or they attained final *nibbāna* (that is, died) a few days later (Mil 264ff.). Did they not necessarily become renouncers in the very moment they became Arahants? If so, they had no reason to stay at home. Thus the Buddha's father, Suddhodana, attained final *nibbāna* soon after becoming an Arahant. Yasa and Khemā, on the other hand, joined the monastic Community. Although rare, such examples show that, according to Theravāda Buddhism, laypeople could become

Arahants. Thus originally the Pali expression *sāvaka saṅgha,* "the community of disciples" (literally "hearers") was employed in canonical texts to designate all those disciples, lay or monastic, who had reached one of the four stages on the Path of Liberation.

Lay Life Compared to Monastic Life

Is it easy or difficult to reach the goal set by Buddhism while leading the life of a lay person? In theory, Theravāda Buddhism asserts that lay people can attain the highest degrees of inner progress. In practice, it makes no secret of the difficulties that anyone in the midst of everyday worries would encounter on the path of inner progress. These difficulties do not make it impossible; they do however present a major obstacle. According to the Pali texts, the Buddha had monastic life in mind when he praised inner progress. Everybody knows that an examination is easier to pass for a full-time living-in student than for a part-time external one!

The *Kapila-sutta* (Sn 274) considered the monastic life to be truly superior. In another passage from the *Sutta-nipāta* (221), monks are compared to swans flying high in the sky, while laypeople are compared to brightly-colored, proud peacocks, who are obviously unable to fly as freely as swans. The Buddha said in the *Aṅguttura-nikāya* (I 80):

> Monks, there are two kinds of happiness. Which are they? The happiness of domestic life and that of monastic life. Of the two, the happiness of monastic life is superior.

In the *Ariyapariyesana-sutta* (M I 162), the Buddha distinguishes two kinds of quest: the noble quest (*ariyā pariyesanā*) and the common quest. Someone who sought the incomparable and eternal inner peace of *nibbāna* is engaged in the noble quest, whereas someone who sought a wife, a son, familial and domestic things, was engaged in the common quest. The *Pabbajjā-sutta* (Sn 405) gives the following reason for the *bodhisatta*'s renunciation: "Life in the home is an obstacle, it is the way of passions; life outside is the life of freedom." Other passages from the Canon enlarged on this idea (e.g. M II 54, S II 219, D I 63). When Yasa came to the Buddha, disparaging domestic life as a "distress" and a "calamity," the Buddha described monastic life to him thus: "Yasa, here is the absence of distress, the absence of calamity" (Vin I 15). Many stories emphasize the superiority of the monastic life preached by the Buddha.

On the one hand, the Buddha gave advice to lay people on how to obtain success and happiness. On the other hand, he did not grant the highest value to family life, but insisted on the superiority of monastic life. Is there not a contradiction here? The answer lies in the Buddha's teaching method. In the *Pahārāda-sutta* (A IV 197, Ud p.53, Vin II 237), the Buddha compares his Doctrine to the ocean in order to illustrate how his teaching gradually gains depth. Those who wished could venture out into the ocean, and dive into it in search of precious stones and pearls, but those who preferred could stay near the beach, swimming and looking for shells. In the same way, the Doctrine was not reserved exclusively for those who were intent on reaching the highest stages of inner progress. It is also meant for ordinary people, who tried to put into practice the Buddha's advice on how to gain happiness in their daily life. The Buddha declared on several occasions (cf. M I 379, III 1, A III 215–218): "Monks, in this Doctrine and in this Discipline, there is gradual instruction, gradual training, gradual action, gradual teaching and gradual method."

His way of conversing with visitors illustrates this gradual approach. He would start the conversation with friendly talk; then he would recall the benefits which accrue to those who practice alms-giving, to those who practice moral values, and the rewards which they will reap in heaven. If his visitor seemed interested, the Master would then speak of the misery, vanity and defilement born of sensual pleasures, and contrast them with the happiness brought about by renouncing such pleasures. The canonical texts refer to this way of conversing as the gradual teaching of the Buddha (cf.D I 110, II 41; M I 379; A IV 207; Vin I 15).

After a discussion of this kind, a young man from a distinguished family called Raṭṭhapāla expressed himself in the following words:

> If I understand rightly what the Blessed One said, it is not easy for someone who stays in his home to lead the religious life in its fullness, in its absolute purity, polished as a conch-shell.
>
> (M II 54)[5]

Here Buddhism did not completely condemn lay life; it only asserted that it was more difficult for ordinary lay people to follow the path of inner progress. In this sense, canonical texts do not contradict themselves on the subject. They constantly emphasize the superiority of monastic life and underline the misery, vanity, defilement and precariousness of sensual pleasures, in opposition to the happiness brought about by renouncing these pleasures. If, however, people wished to remain in family life, canonical texts gave them advice on how to live happy and honestly with their fellows.

The responsibilities and preoccupations of lay life were thought to make it more difficult for people to grasp the fundamental ideas of the Doctrine. When Anāthapiṇḍika, the Buddha's greatest devotee, was on his deathbed, the venerable Sāriputta Thera, accompanied by the venerable Ānanda Thera, came and preached to him. He spoke on deep and metaphysical subjects; Anāthapiṇḍika wept, saying that he had never heard such a discourse, despite the fact that he had been a supporter of the Buddha and his monks for many years. Sāriputta then told him that laity did not understand such discourses, that only members of the monastic Order could understand them; however, Anāthapiṇḍika begged Sāriputta to expound such intricate sermons to laity as well, for there would be some who would understand (M III 264, S V 380–389). The *Sigālovāda-sutta* (D III 180) mentions as one of the monks' six duties towards lay people that they should show them "the way to heaven." The way to deliverance, the way to *nibbāna*, on the other hand, was thought to be more difficult to grasp, even at the time of the Buddha. Both texts illustrate the Buddhist position with respect to lay religion; two levels were distinguished: laypeople strove for merit, monks and nuns strove for inner progress towards non-attachment. This is why an anthropological approach to Buddhist religion can distinguish "two Buddhisms" in Theravāda: *nibbanic Buddhism*, which demands absolute renunciation and encourages its followers to attain the state of Arahant as soon as possible, and *kammatic Buddhism*, which concerns meritorious acts and abstaining from demeritorious ones.[6] (For these "two kinds" of Buddhism, see the *Mahācattārīsaka Sutta*).

It was obviously in the hope of gaining good results that lay people performed meritorious acts: notably, they hoped for good rebirth in the cycle of *samsāra*. Of course, lay people could also hope to reach the state of Arahant, but without seeking to attain it as soon as possible: they accepted the fact that leading a family life made it difficult for them to commit themselves with any depth to renunciation and inner progress. They put deliverance from *samsāra* in second place, and took good rebirth as their immediate goal. They preferred a rebirth rich in sensual pleasures; for ordinary lay people, this was an easier goal to contemplate than *nibbāna*. This does not mean, however, that lay followers completely rejected *nibbāna;* on the contrary, they hoped one day to have the opportunity to attain it more easily, but after having tasted the pleasures of heaven. While accepting *nibbāna* as the final goal of Buddhism, they did not regard it as their immediate objective, whereas for monks and nuns (unless they wanted to become *bodhisattas*, and thus eventually Buddhas themselves) *nibbāna* constituted both the immediate and the final goal.

In the canonical texts dealing with inner progress, no advice is found concerning meritorious acts, rewards in heaven and happy rebirths. On the other hand, many discourses addressed to laity insist on meritorious acts. The *Nikaya* texts include several lists showing the everyday expectations of lay people who performed meritorious acts: wealth, good reputation, a long life, happy rebirth (A III 45); a long life, beauty, happiness, physical strength (S V 387); beauty, happiness, good reputation, happy rebirth (A III 47). Various well-known discourses give the following advice:

> Householder, there are five benefits that accrue to a man who performs meritorious acts and practices morality: the first benefit is that he acquires his wealth by honest means; the second that he acquires a good reputation; the third that he can appear without hesitation before any gathering, whether of noblemen or brahmins, of householders or monks; the fourth that he will die without anxiety; the fifth, finally, that he will have a good rebirth in heaven. These are, householder, the five benefits earned by the man who performs meritorious acts.
>
> (D II 85–86, III 235–236; A III 252; Ud 86; Vin I 227)

These discourses illustrate many aspects of lay religion: the objectives they list are the same as those which people wished to attain through the performance of domestic or royal sacrifices, as was prescribed by orthodox Brahmanism. In a Buddhist society, however, brahmanical sacrifices were replaced by the notion of *kamma,* and lay followers turned their attention to gaining merit and abstaining from misdeeds which only brought unhappiness.

There is another noteworthy aspect of this form of Buddhism: for lay followers encouraged to earn merit, the Buddha's Community of disciples appeared as "the incomparable field of merit" (e.g. D III 5; M I 446, III 80; A I 244, II 34, and in very many other places). Ordinary lay followers were to sow their meritorious acts in this field in order to gain the best "harvests": the reward of their meritorious acts. This is how Buddhism became "kammatic Buddhism" for ordinary lay followers. Wealthy Buddhists such as Anāthapiṇḍika, Meṇḍaka, Visākhā, and others made donations to the Community, and other lay followers imitated them. Instead of spending their money on sacrifices, now they spent in on gaining merit, notably by making donations to monks and nuns. The enthusiasm of lay followers for gaining merit was closely related to their willingness to support the Buddha's Community of disciples.

The Place of Lay People in Buddhism

It is true that canonical texts most often give pride of place to members of the monastic Community. The Pali *Vinaya-piṭaka* is exclusively devoted to monastic discipline. At the start of many discourses from the *Sutta-piṭaka*, the Buddha addressed monks, and most of his advice concerned detachment, renunciation, and similar subjects. At first sight, the Pali texts do not accord much importance to lay people, and this explains why some authors have characterized Theravāda Buddhism as a monastic religion, and Mahāyāna Buddhism as more concerned with lay people. The Mahāyāna ideal, the *bodhisattva* (Pali *bodhisatta*), is not essentially a monastic figure, but on the contrary, very often a lay person. Although Theravādins accept with enthusiasm the *bodhisatta* ideal, they attach equal value to the ideal of Arahant, which is a monastic ideal. Both Theravāda and Mahāyāna Buddhism agree that the historical Buddha was not a layman, but a monk. Renunciation is an essential value for Mahāyāna Buddhism too.

In Theravāda Buddhism, members of the monastic Community have enjoyed a higher status than lay followers. On close inspection, however, it does not appear that lay people were neglected, or that Theravāda Buddhism is a religion restricted to monks and nuns. It is obvious in the Canon that Buddhism was not a philosophy or a cult isolated and separated from lay society. On the contrary, it evolved with lay people, in their midst, with their collaboration, and as much for their benefit as for that of monks and nuns. Although laity are not given first place in the Pali *Vinaya*, they are never absent from it, and always appear alongside members of the monastic Community. They constantly intervened in the affairs of the Community, as its protectors, critics and donors. In Theravāda Buddhism, without lay followers the monastic

Community could not exist. Monks were not, it is true, allowed to let them take part in regulatory acts of the Community (Vin I 115), but if they could not participate in the Community's gatherings, and if they were not prescribed very strict precepts, it was not because they were considered unworthy. Monks and nuns were treated as monks and nuns, and lay people were treated as lay people, each given a place according to their choice, their abilities, their possibilities, their wishes. The choice was open: one could either become a monk or a nun in order to practice the highest principles, or remain a lay follower obeying simpler precepts and principles. In this new religion without priests, lay followers enjoyed a greater liberty. Monks and nuns had no authority to control lay people or to excommunicate them.

According to the *Mahāparinibbāna-sutta* (D II 160), the arrangements for the Buddha's funeral were entrusted only to lay followers, in accordance with the Buddha's expressed wish before his death: it is important that he should have wanted his lay disciples, not his religious disciples, to deal with his funeral. After the funeral, lay followers are said to have shared his relics between themselves (D II 165); no monk or nun, Arahant or non-Arahant, was to distribute or request any relics of the departed Master. This story by itself allows us to assess the difference which existed in Theravāda Buddhist thought between lay and monastic religion.

Endnotes

1. The first two converts, Tapassu and Bhallika, were only able to take two refuges, the Buddha and his Teaching, since the monastic Community had not yet come into existence (Vin I 4). The first person to take the Three Refuges was Yasa's father (Vin I 18).
2. [See Appendix 3.]
3. See G.P.Malalasekara, *Buddhism and the Racial Question*, Unesco, 1968.
4. [See Appendix 3.]

5. For several centuries now lay people from Theravāda countries such as Thailand and Burma have followed the custom of joining the monastic Community temporarily: for a short period of a few days, a few weeks or a few months. Undergoing even such a short period of monastic training is thought to facilitate inner progress in a future life. Besides, Buddhists hold the view that maturity is fully attained only after some time has been spent in a monastery, under the guidance of monks. This custom has come to have a particular social significance: parents wishing to marry their daughter take notice of it and often distrust a young man who has not spent some time in a monastery: in their eyes, he has not reached maturity. The practice has become widespread nationally: even the Thai king, for example, entered the monastic Community for a period of three months in 1956.
6. [These terms were introduced by M.E.Spiro (70) See bibliography in the Introduction.]

Appendix 3

The precepts (sikkhāpadāni)

Buddhist novices and postulants have undertaken to observe between five and ten of the following list of Precepts. Each is preceded by the words "I undertake to observe the precept to abstain from":

1. killing
2. stealing ("taking what is not given")
3. sexual relations
4. telling lies
5. drinking liquor that causes intoxication and heedlessness
6. eating after noon
7. {7. dancing, singing, music and unseemly shows
   {8. using garlands, perfumes and unguents; and things which tend to beautify and adorn the person
8./ 9. using high and luxurious seats and beds
10. handling money.

In the past, postulant nuns undertook to observe 1–6 for two years (see p.135 n.3); in the past female novices, and both then and nowadays male novices and some lay people, have taken 1–10 (here the eighth in the *Uposatha* day list is divided into two). Lay people on *Uposatha* days can take 1–8 (all except 10; see pp.170–1); all lay Buddhists take 1, 2, 4 and 5; their third precept is to abstain from illicit or improper sexual relations, rather than complete abstinence.

Glossary

ācariya – teacher

aḍḍhayoga – a round residence, one of the five allowed to monks

adhikaraṇa samatha – procedural rules

āmisa dāna – material gifts (from laity to monks or nuns)

anāgāmi – see *sotāpanna*

anattā – without self

anicca – impermanent

aniyata – offence whose classification is not determined (cf. p.141)

antaravāsaka – one of the three robes, worn as underclothing

antarāyikā dhammā – obstructions

āpatti – fault, offense

arhat, arahant – see *sotāpanna*

ayyā – "noble lady," form of address for nuns

bhāvanā – meditation, spiritual development

bhikkhu – monk

bhikkhunī – nun

bodhisatta – future Buddha

brahmacariya – "the holy life," celibacy

brahmadaṇḍa – a form of punishment, in which other monks and nuns refuse to speak to an offender against the rules

cattaro parisā – four-fold assembly (monks, nuns, laymen and women)

cātuddisa saṅgha – "the Community of the Four Quarters" (referring to the *Saṅgha* as a whole, without reference to particular persons)

citta-viveka – mental detachment

dukkha – unsatisfactory, suffering

dhamma – the Buddha's Teaching, the Truth

dhamma dāna – "gift of the Truth" (preaching or teaching by monks and nuns)

dhutaṅga – ascetic practice

eka-vihāri – one who lives alone (physically or psychologically)

gahapati-cīvara – robes given by householders

gaṇa – group (of ascetics)

gaṇācariya – teacher/leader of a *gaṇa*

hammiya – a monastic residence with more than one story

jātarūparajata – gold and silver, money

jhāna – (stage of) meditation

kahāpaṇa – a coin, an amount of money

kaṇḍupaṭichādi – piece of cloth allowed for use with skin diseases

kappiya-kāraka – "one who makes suitable": a lay-servant of a monastery, who accepts gifts which monks cannot accept directly on their behalf *kaṭhina-cīvara* – robes given by laity at the end of the Rainy Season Retreat

kaṭhina-vattha – material used for *kaṭhina-cīvara*

kāsāya-vatthāni – yellow robes

kaya-bandhana – a strip of cloth used as a belt

kāya-viveka – bodily detachment, physical solitude

mānatta– a temporary probation

māsaka – a coin, an amount of money

mūgavatta – "vow of dumbness," taken by non-Buddhist ascetics

muni – sage

nibbāna – freedom from rebirth, salvation

nissaggiya pācittiya – offence requiring confession and forfeiture of what has been improperly obtained

nissaya – dependence (see p.147)

pabbajjā – "Going Forth," the Minor Ordination (cf. *upasampadā*)

pabbajjanīya kamma – legal act of expulsion from a monastic dwelling

pācittiya – offence requiring confession

pāda – a coin, an amount of money

pakāsanīya kamma – legal act imposed on Devadatta (see p.156 n.6)

paṃsukūla-cīvara – rag-robes

pāpa-, puñña-kamma – (de)meritorious action

pārājika – offense entailing defeat

paribbājaka – wandering religious mendicant

parivāsa – (period of) probation

pasāda – long residence, one of the five allowed to monks

pāṭidesanīya – lesser offence requiring confession

pātimokkha – the Disciplinary Code

paṭisāraṇīya kamma – legal act of reconciliation, where a monk or nun asks forgiveness for a fault

pavāraṇā – ceremony of confession of faults (between monks), held at the end of the Rainy Season Retreat

piṭaka – Basket (of Scripture)

puthujjana – "ordinary person," who has not reached *sotāpanna* status

ṛṣi – seer

saddhivihārika – "one who lives with," a pupil living with a preceptor

saddutiya vihāri – "one who lives with a second" (physically or psychologically)

sakadāgāmi – see *sotāpanna*

samakaccikā – under-vest worn by nuns

sāmaṇera/sāmaṇerī – male/female novice

sammuti-vajjā – conventional offences (i.e. infractions of the monastic Rule, not necessarily against universal moral rules)

saṃsāra – rebirth

saṅgha – the monastic Community

saṅgha-bheda – schism in a Community

saṅghādisesa – offence which must be judged by a formal meeting of the Community

saṅgha-kamma (= *vinaya-kamma*) – legal act of the Community

saṅghāṭi – outer robe

saṅgīti – communal recitation, Council

saraṇāgamana – going for refuge (to the Buddha, Dhamma and Saṅgha)

sāvaka-saṅgha – community of disciples (monastic or lay) who had reached one of the four stages on the Path (cf. *sotāpanna*, etc.)

sekhiyā – training precepts, precepts of good behaviour

sikkhamānā – female postulant

sikkhāpadāni – Precepts

sotāpanna – "one who has entered the Stream", the first of the four stages of the Path (the others are: *sakadāgāmi*, "once-returner, *anāgāmi*, "non-returner," and *arhat*, liberated "Saint"; cf. pp.160, 172)

tāpasa – ascetic

tathāgata – a title for the Buddha

tevijjā – three-fold knowledge (see p.163 n.4)

thera, therī – monk/nun of ten years' standing

theyyasaṃvāsaka – a "usurper," one who wears the robe without valid ordination

ubhato-saṅgha – two-fold Community (of monks and nuns)

udaka-sāṭikā – bathing-robe allowed to nuns

ukkhepanīya kamma – legal act imposing punishments on an offender

upadhi-viveka – "detachment from substrates" (synonym for *nibbāna*)

upāsaka, upāsikā – male/female lay follower

upasampadā – Major Ordination

uposatha – monastic ceremony taking place every half-month, at which the *Pātimokkha* is recited *uposathāgāra* – hall where the *Pātimokkha* is recited

upajjhāya – preceptor

uttara-saṅga – inner robe

vassa – Rainy Season (Retreat)

vihāra – monastery, monastic dwelling

vihāra-cīvara – robes left by laity in monasteries for future use

vinaya – Discipline

Index